RAMAVIJAYA

(THE MYTHOLOGICAL HISTORY OF RAMA.)

With Illustrations.

GYAN

Published by

Gyan Publishing House
5, Ansari Road
Daryaganj, New Delhi-110002
Phone: 011-47034999, 9811692060
E-mail: books@gyanbooks.com

Distribution Network
gyanbooks.com
India, USA, Canada, UK, Australia, France

ISBN: 978-81-212-8959-7 (PB)
First Published, 1891

2nd Impression 2023

Printed at: Gyan Press, Delhi.

RAMAVIJAYA

RAMAVIJAYA

RAMAVIJAYA.

(THE MYTHOLOGICAL HISTORY OF RAMA.)

With Illustrations.

Bombay

DUBHASHI & Co.,

GIRGAUM BACK ROAD.

1891

RAMAVIJAYA.

THE MYTHOLOGICAL HISTORY OF RAMA.

———O———

Powlasti, a son of *Bramhadev*,* was married to Devavarni, and he had a son called Vishrava. A daughter of Bharadwaja, a *Rishi*,† was given away in marriage to Vishrava; and she had a son called Kuber. Bramhadev had created Lanka and given it to Kuber. While Kuber was ruling there, a demon came from *Patal* ‡ in the form of a Brahman and became very jealous of him. The demon said to himself, "Lanka is my country and this man has no right to rule here." So saying to himself he gave away his daughter, Kakesi, in marriage to Vishrava with a view to drive out Kuber of his country, Lanka, with the help of the sons who would be born to her by him. Vishrava had got by Kakesi three demons, Ravana, Kumbhakarna, and Vibhishana and two demonesses, Tateka and Surpanakha. Ravan and his brothers went to Gokarna, where they performed severe penances. *Siva*§ was propitiated by Ravana, Bramhadev by Kumbhakarna, and *Vishnu*¶ by Vibhishana. Bramhadev was pleased with them and called upon them to ask him for blessings. Ravana was blessed with a power to imprison all gods and also with wealth and learning. Kumbhakarna wanted such a blessing from Bramhadev as would enable him to devour heaven and earth. All the gods were, therefore, alarmed and prayed to the goddess, Saraswati, who induced the demon to ask the god for sleep. Bramhadev blessed

---

* The creating god of the universe. † A sage. ‡ The regions under the earth. § The destroying god of the universe. ¶ The protecting god of the universe.

him with sleep, saying that the demon would rise every six months to eat his meals and indulge in all other luxuries. Vibhishana was blessed with a power to pray always to Vishnu. Ravana and Kumbhakarana then collected all demons including Kharadushana and Trishira and marched against Kuber to conquer Lanka. They fought with Kuber with bravery, but the latter repulsed them with heavy loss. Ravana then went to Vishrava and brought his letter to Kuber asking him to give Lanka to the demon without any resistance. On reading the letter from his father he gave the country to Ravana and proceeded to heaven by a *Viman.** Mayasur, a demon, gave away his daughter, Mandodari, in marriage to Ravana. Dirghajwala, a grand-daughter of Bali, was married to Kumbhakarna, and Sharma, a daughter of a *Gandharv,*† to Vibhishana. Ravana conquered all countries and devoured a large number of Brahmans and cows. He robbed Kuber of his treasure and oppressed all other people. He had eight thousand wives. one lac of sons and one lac and twenty thousand grand-sons. He had eighteen *kshoyanis*‡ of musicians, who entertained him with music. All kings were his slaves, and eight thousand torches lighted his *sabha* § every night. All mountains for fear of *Indra* ¶ prayed to Ravana for protection, who told them to become elephants. They accordingly became elephants whom he engaged as his servants. He then marched against Indra with his eldest son, Meghanand. A severe battle took place between the gods and the demons, but the former were defeated by the latter. In that battle Meghanand flung down Indra with his *hairawati,*$ and

---

* A conveynance or a chariot serving as a throne through the skies, self-directed and self-moving. † A demi-god. ‡ One kshoyani consists of 21,870 chariots, 21,870 elephants, 1,09,350 foot, and 65,610 horses. § A court. ¶ The king of the gods. $ An elephant.

hence he was called Indrajit, the conquerer of Indra. All the gods were seized by Ravana and released on the condition that they should serve him in his household in different capacities. All the gods became his slaves; Indra served him as his butler, Chandra held a *chatra** over him, Kuber and Anil cleaned and washed all the things in his house. Agni served him as his washerman, and Gabhasti as his page. Brahaspati was his pleader, Bramhadev his priest, and Narada always entertained him with singing. Ravana became a great favourite of Siva; and by his blessing he had got ten faces and twenty hands. One day he, proud of his prosperity, went by his viman to Kailasa, the place of Siva, when *Nandi*,† who was guarding the door of the abode in which the god lived, prevented him from entering it. The demon was greatly insulted at the conduct of Nandi, and said "I do not care a fig of thee and thy master." So saying he began to force his way in, when Siva cursed him and said to him, "A human being and monkeys will kill thee in a battle." Enraged at this curse he tried to pull off the mountain on which the abode of Siva stood with a view to carry it to Lanka, when the god pressed it in such a manner that the domon-king was confined to it for one thousand years. He always cried and prayed to Siva during the time for his release. One day the god pitied him and set him free. Thence he went to Sahasrarjun and praised his own strength there, when the latter caught hold of him and put him in his arms. He was ashamed and went to the kingdom of Bali, who possessed prodigious strength. He entered the palace of the king and praised his valour and bravery, when the latter said in order to test his strength, "There lie the *kundalas* ‡ of the demon, Heranyakashapu, whom Vishnu had killked to protect Pralada. Just go and get the

* A large and lofty parasol. † The bull on which Siva rides.
‡ Ear-ornaments.

ornaments here." Ravana went to bring them but he could not lift them up, when Bali said to him, "If thou canst bring the kundalas, just get that die which fell down there, while my wife and I were playing together." Ravana accordingly went to bring the die but, to his great surprise, he could not remove it, when both Bali and his wife heartily laughed at him. Ravana, humbled as he was, set out for Lanka; but on the road he was robbed of his clothes and ornaments and let off with soot being applied to his ten faces and with his hands tied up behind like a prisoner. He was much troubled by the people on the road. Some threw dust at him, some slapped him in the face, some pulled him by the beard and others made him sit down on a dung-hill. A maid-servant of Bali caught him so forcibly that he implored her to spare his life. Vishrava then came there and begged of Bali to make a present of the demon to him. His request was granted and Ravana was let off. The demon-king returned to Lanka with shame and confusion. A few days after his return to Lanka he went to catch Vali, who carried him away in his arms to his house and tied him up to the cradle in which his son, Angada, was fast asleep. Vishrava came and requested Vali to set him free. Vali granted his request and, applying soot to all the faces of Ravana, allowed him to go to Lanka. One day he asked Bramhadev to inform him by whose hands he would die, when the god told him that he would die by the hands of Rama, a son of Dasharatha and grand-son of Ajapal. Ravana got very indignant and said that he would kill Dasharatha and his wife by any means. Soon after, Ajapal made preparations for celebrating the marriage of his son with Kausalya, when Narada told him to watch his son and daughter-in-law, because Ravana would kill them under any circumstances. Whereupon Ajapal took Dasharatha and Kausalya on board a ship in the sea far off and was about to tell his priest to perform their marriage, when Ravana attacked the ship at night with a large army of demons and broke her in the sea. All perished except Dasharatha and Kausalya. Ravana put Kausalya into a box and handed it over to a fish, which carried it to a desolate island and deposited it there for safety. Dasharatha struggled much with the waves of the sea but at last he got into a broken vessel, which was carried by the waves to the island, where the box was deposited by the fish. Dasharatha landed on the sea-shore ; and seeing the box there he seated himself upon it for rest. Having got refreshed, he opened the box out of curiosity but, to his great surprise, he found Kausalya in it. Narada came there in the meantime and, having perfomed their marriage, blessed them, saying that the god, Rama, would be born to them. In Lanka Ravana asked the god, Bramhadev, about his prediction. . He said to the god, " Where is Dasharatha? You know, he has already perished in the sea." Bramhadev replied, "Long since Dasharatha has been married to Kausalya; and you will see that Rama will be shortly born to them." Ravana said, " Well then, get them here." Bramhadev replied, " If I get them here, what will you give me ?" Ravana said, "I promise to give you whatever you will ask from me." Bramhadev then went and brought the box from the island and, having opened it, he showed the bride and bridegroom to the demon. As soon as he saw them, he got exceedingly enraged and was about to cut off their heads, when Bramhadev stepped forward and said to him, " You promised me that you would give me whatever I would ask from you. I, therefore, ask you not to kill Dasharatha and Kausalya." Ravana replied, " You may ask me for any other thing but I cannot spare the lives of those wretched beings." Bramhadev said, " I do not want any other hings from you but I want you to spare their lives." Ravana could not break his promise and accordingly spared their lives. Bramhadev then brought them to Ayodya and placed Dasharatha on the throne of the country. One day while Ravana was going by his viman, he observed on the road a beautiful woman, who was the wife of a god and sought to outrage her modesty. She complained to Bramhadev against the conduct of the demon, when the god cursed him and said that if he would outrage the modesty of any woman, he would be cut into one hundred pieces. For fear of the curse he let her go and began to devour the Brahmans and cows that came in his way. The earth trembled and went in the form of a cow to Bramhadev with all the gods and Rishis and applied to him for protection, when a voice said, "I will be born in the family of Dasharatha and called Rama; and killing Ravana and all other demons, I will make all the gods and good people happy. For the purpose of helping me the *Shesha* * on which I lie, will be my second brother, who will be named Lakshuman, the *shankha*,† which is in my hand, will be my third brother, who will be called Bharata and the *sudarshan*,‡ my weapon, will be my fourth brother, who will be named Shatrughana; and ye, all the gods, will be monkeys. Siva will be Maruti; Bramhadev, Janbuvant; Dhanavantari, Sushen; Brahasapati, Angada; the sun, Sugriva; Agni, Nala; and Yama, Rashabha." Listening to the voice of Vishnu all the gods and Rishis were glad and returned to their respective places. At Ayodya Dasharatha married more wives, Sumitra and Kayakayi. He was an accomplished prince and very dexterous in the use of *dhanushabans*.§ One day he dreamt a dream in which he found that he had killed an innocent man and woman. Whereupon he asked his *guru*,¶ Vashista, a Rishi, to interprete

* The king of the serpent-race, as a large, thousand headed snakes, at once the couch and canopy of Vishnu and the upholder of the world which rests on one of its heads. † The conch-shell. ‡ A discus. § Bows and arrows. ¶ A spiritual teacher

See Page 7.
DASHARATHA
SHRAVAN
FATHER
MOTHER
See Page 16
KINGS.
RISHIS.

the dream, when the latter said to him, "This dream indicates bad omens. I, therefore, advise you to kill a few stags and perform a penance, so that nothing bad may happen to you." Listening to the advice of the guru Dasharatha went to a forest for hunting stags; and though he worked hard the whole day, he did not come across any stag. At the sun-set he lay in wait at a lake anxiously expecting a stag there. But, in the meantime, a man called Shravan came there with a *kavada** across his shoulders in which his helpless old mother and father were seated by him. His parents, being thirsty, asked their son to fetch some water for them. Whereupon Shravan placed the kavada on the ground, and taking a goblet in his hand, went to the lake; but whilst he was taking the water, the king took him for a stag and discharged an arrow at him, which passed through his heart. Dasharatha came where he was lying and became extremely sorry for the accident, when Shravan said to him, "I shall not now live. Please, therefore, take some water in this goblet and give it to my parents, as they are very thirsty; and as soon as I hear that they have quenched their thirst, I shall instantly die. They are very old and cannot walk. I carry them in a kavada across my shoulder. Oh, my good king, take care of these poor creatures. There is no one to look after them." Dasharatha sighed and wept but the loss was irreparable. The king then took some water in the goblet and stood where the kavada was placed without speaking a word. The old woman and the man, who were blind, taking him for Shravan, said, "Child, why doest thou not speak? Art thou angry with us, because we sent thee to the lake at this hour? Child, thou art always obedient to us and what has irritated thee today?" These words made Dasharatha shed tears, and at

* A bamboo lath provided with slings at each end for the conveyance across the shoulder of pitcher, &c.

last he broke the sad news to the old parents of Shravan, when they cried violently and said, "Shravan, none can get a son like thee in this world. We feel much for thee and die with thee. Oh, we cannot bear this grief. You, the murderer of our child, we curse you and say that you will also die of grief for your son in the same way we do." So saying they instantly expired. Dasharatha grieved much for Shravan and his old parents whom he had killed by his own hands, and performed their funeral ceremonies. The king then returned to Ayodya and informed Vashista of what had happened. At this time there was a great famine in the country, as there was no rain for twelve years; and consequently the subjects of the king died of thirst and hunger one after another. The rain was stopped, because Vrashaparva, a powerful demon, fought with the gods in heaven with the assistance of his guru, Shukra. Indra, therefore, sent a chariot to Dasharatha and requested him to come up to heaven and kill the demon, informing him at the same time, that the rain was stopped on account of the battle with the gods. Whereupon Dasharatha went by the chariot to Indra with his favourit wife, Kayakayi. Immediately on his arrival there Dasharatha fought with the demons and killed a large number of them, when Vrashaparva made an attack upon the king but he was also repulsed. His guru, Shukra, then took the field and discharged arrows at the king, when the chariot of the king was about to give way but his wife, Kayakayi, supported it by one of her hands, of which the king knew nothing. Dasharatha bravely continued the fight and cut off the guru's horse and *mugut.** Shukra fled in alarm with the other demons. When every thing was over, the king was informed that the victory he had gained in the battle with the demons, was due to his wife, Kayakayi. The king was pleased with her, and asked her what reward she

* A Tiaria.

wanted from him. Kayakayi replied, " Kindly give me your promise that you will give me whatever I will ask from you; and I shall ask you for it whenever I like." The king generously gave the promise she required.

The victory, gained by Dasharatha in the battle with the demons, was due to Kayakayi, because when she was young, a *Tapaswi** came to her parents and stayed with them for a day. At the time of his bathing her mother told her to go and rub his body with scents. She accordingly went to him with the scents; but finding that the Tapaswi was absorbed in meditation, she applied soot to his face instead of the scents. Having found that the soot had been applied to his face, he got indignant and cursed the doer of the mischeif and said. " Whoever has applied this soot to my face, will always be looked upon by all people with contempt." Her mother was afraid of this curse; and finding that it was her daughter's doing, she threw herself at the feet of the Tapaswi and implored him to make the curse a little milder. Whereupon the Tapaswi said, " The hand with which your daughter has applied the soot to my face, will give success to her husband in a battle which he will fight with demons and for which only she will be praised by all."

After the battle was over, Brahasapti asked the king whether he had any issue. Dasharatha replied, " I am very sorry that I have no issue." The god blessed him and said, " Vishnu, the protecting god of the universe, will be born to you." Indra said, " There is a Rishi called Shringa Rishi, who has not yet seen a human face. He lives with his father in a forest; and if he is induced and brought to Ayodya, his father, who is a great Tapaswi, will come there in search of his son; and by his blessing you will get children. I shall, therefore, send a *devangana* †

* An ascetic. † The wife of a god.

to the forest to charm him with her beauty and singing, so that he may easily follow her." Dasharatha thanked Indra and returned to Ayodya with Kayakayi. Indra accordingly sent a devangana to the forest. The young Rishi was placed by his father, Vibhandak, on a *mala* * in order that he might not be devoured by lions and tigers. The young boy, having seen the woman, was at first frightened; but soon after, he was charmed with her beauty and singing. As his father was absent, she brought him to Ayodya. Dasharatha cordially received him; and shortly after, he gave away his foster-daughter in marriage to him. Vibhandak knew by his *yoga*† that his son was taken to Ayodya in his absence, and got so much enraged that he immediately went to that city to curse the woman to death. Dasharatha treated him with respect; and on finding that his son was married to the foster-daughter of the king, he was pleased with him and blessed him, saying that four mighty sons would be born to him. The Rishi then made a *havan*.‡ The god, Agni, came out of it and entrusted to Vashista a *thali* § full of *payas* ¶ and told him to divide it equally among the three wives of the king, so that they might get sons, as soon as they partook of it. Vashista made three *pindas* $ of the payas and gave the largest of them to Kausalya, the eldest wife of Dasharatha, and the other two to Sumitra and Kayakayi. Kayakayi, the third wife of the king, became jealous and said that she was entitled to the largest pinda, because she supported the chariot of the king by her own hands, which was about to give way during the battle with the demons. While she was thus quarreling about it, a *ghar* ‖ from above snatched the pinda from her hands and flew in the

* An erected seat. † A union with Bramha through abstract meditation. ‡ A large hole made in the ground for receiving and preserving consecrated fire. § A cooking pot. ¶ A dish composed of rice, sugar, milk, &c. $ Lumps. ‖ A kite.

air with it. She became exceedingly sorry and began to weep, when Dasharatha prevailed upon Kausalya to divide her pinda into two halves and give one to Kayakayi and keep the other for herself. Kausalya accordingly did it; and Sumitra also did the same thing in compliance with the wishes of the king. Thus Kayakayi got one full pinda for herself, which she ate heartily. Kausalya and Sumitra ate their own halves. Soon after, the three ladies became pregnant. The pinda which was snatched by the ghar from the hands of Kayakayi, fell by a blast of wind into the hands of Anjani, the wife of a monkey called Kesari. She also swallowed up the pinda and became pregnant. The story of the child born to Anjani is as follows:—

Anjani, the wife of Kesari, performed a severe penance for seven years on the hills called Rishiparvat, in order that the god, Siva, might be pleased to bless her with an immortal son. Siva was pleased with her and said, "An immortal son will be born to thee as thou wishest. He will be a part of my body. I, therefore, tell thee to sit here in meditation and swallow up any thing that falls into thy hands, so that thy wish may be fulfilled." So saying Siva dis-appeared. The pinda from the bill of the ghar fell into the hands of Anjani, and she swallowed it up as directed by Siva.

The ghar was a devangana who had become a bird by the curse of Indra. This god was displeased with her, because she did not dance properly; and it was appointed by Bramhadev that she would be released from the curse, as soon as the pinda fell into the hands of Anjani. The devangana was accordingly released from the curse; and after her release she went to Indra. Anjani, after a period of nine months, was delivered of a powerful son called Maruti He was a monkey and had a long tail. When he saw the light, he was hungry; and when he did not get any thing to eat, he went to devour the sun, taking him for a fruit. At that time Rahu also came there to devour the sun, when Maruti said to him, "Who art thou? I have come here first to devour the fruit." So saying he broke the head of Rahu with his tail and, catching him by his feet, flung him down. Ketu then came to help him, but he was also severely beaten by the monkey. In the mean-time, Maruti was brought down by his father, the wind.

After nine months Kausalya, Sumitra and Kayakayi were delivered of sons. Rama was born to Kausalya; Lakshuman to Sumitra; and the twins, Bharat and Shatrughana to Kayakayi. They grew up, and the ceremonies of investing them with sacred threads were performed. They were taught by Vashista the *Vedas** and *mantras*.† On his return from a pilgrimage Viswamitra, a Rishi, came to Ayodya. Dasharatha received him cordially and worshipped him with devotion. The Rishi blessed him and said to him, "Dasharatha, I want you to give me a promise that you will give me whatever, I will ask from you." The king gave him the promise the Rishi required, when the latter said to the former, "We all the Rishis are very much troubled by the demons, Maricha, Subhahu, and others. They have often destroyed our havans; and consequently we are not able to perform our *yadnya*‡ successfully. No one can kill them except Rama. I therefore, wish you to send Rama with me to kill the demons." Dasharatha was startled and replied, "Rishi, how can I send my tender child with you? How can he kill the mountain-like demons? You may ask me for any other thing but not Rama." Vishwamitra became very indignant and said, "You ought to have considered well, before you gave me the promise. At any rate I must now take Rama with me."

* Sacred writings of the Hindus. † Incantations. ‡ A sacrifice.

In the mean-time Vashista came there and advised the king to send Rama with the Rishi, saying that if he did not listen to him, he would curse him and his sons, as he was obstinate and of a choleric disposition. Dasharatha then brought Rama and Lakshuman before his sabha and gave them in charge of the Rishi. Vishwamitra then accompanied by two young boys, set out for the forest, where the Rishis were performing their yadnya. But on the road they were encountered by Tatika, a hideous and frightful demoness. She had the strength of ten thousand elephants, her chest was as large as a mountain, her hair and dress were saturated with blood, the strings of dead-bodies were put round her neck, and her head was besmeared with *shindur*.* As soon as she saw them, she opened her mouth and went with other demonesses to devour them, when Rama instantly killed her with one arrow. Twenty crores† of demons, headed by Banasur, a very powerful demon, then came upon Rama to revenge the killing of the demoness; but they all were repulsed by him with heavy loss. After the defeat of the demons they proceeded on their journey; and when they came near a *shila*,‡ it began to tremble as soon as the dust from the feet of Rama fell upon it; and no sooner did he touch it with his feet, than it became a beautiful woman who, bowing to Rama, returned to her husband. The story of how the woman became a shila is as follows:—

Bramhadev had a very beautiful daughter, named Ahilya. Many gods and kings requested her father to give her away in marriage to them. But Bramhadev had made a condition that whoever would go round the earth and return within six hours, should marry her without loss of time. Whereupon all the kings and gods, including Indra, went round the earth, but none could return within six hours except Gowtam, a Rishi, to whom Ahilya

* Red powders. † Ten millions. ‡ A flat stone.

was married agreeably to the condition. Indra became very jealous of the Rishi and sought to outrage her modesty. Some time after his marriage he and his wife went to a river with Rishis for ablutions on the day of an eclipse. After their ablutions were over, Gowtam sat there with other Rishis for meditation; and his wife returned home. While she was alone in her abode, Indra went there in the form of her husband and outraged her modesty. In the mean-time, Gowtam returned home; and finding Indra in the abode he cursed him and Ahilya, saying that there would be one thousand ulcers on the body of the god and that his wife would be a shila and remain in that state for sixty thousand years; but that as there was no fault on her part, she would be released from the curse, when Rama would touch her with his feet. Ahilya accordingly became a shila and Indra a peacock with one thousand ulcers on his body. While the god in the form of a peacock was flying about in forests, the other gods prayed to Gowtam for him, who, having been pleased with them, restored Indra to his former state and turned all the ulcers on his body into eyes. After the release of Ahilya from the curse, Vishwamitra proceeded on his journey with Rama and Lakshuman. Shatanand, a son of Ahilya and the priest of the king, Janak, also accompanied him. They all arrived at the city of Mathila and put up at a garden there. At the request of Rama Vishwamitra related the story of the birth of Sita, a daughter of Janak, which is as follows:—

" There was a king called Padamaksha. One day he said to Lakshumi, wife of Vishnu, ' I wish you would be born in my family and become my daughter.' She replied, 'If I be born in your family and I become your daughter, you will be miserable. I have however no objection to become your daughter, if my husband tell me to do so.' Whereupon the king performed a severe penance to gain the favour of Vishnu, who was pleased with him and gave him a fruit, which the king took at home and kept with him. After nine months were over, the fruit bore a female child, the same Lakshumi. The king, having got a daughter, became exceedingly glad and named the child Padmakshi. She grew up and became marriageable. Many kings, demi-gods and Rishis requested her father to give her away in marriage to them, but he refused to comply with their request, saying that he would marry her to a man whose body was dark blue. At this refusal they all got enraged and killed the king on the spot. Whereupon his daughter threw herself into a havan in which the consecrated fire was burning. At that time Ravan happened to look at her, and was captivated with her charms. He immediately extinguished the fire with a view to catch her, but she disappeared. He found in the havan five *ratnas*,* which he gave to his wife, Mandodari. The five ratnas were placed by Ravana and his wife in a box; and soon after, they found, to their great surprise, that a female-child played in it with pleasure. Ravana lifted the child, but Mandodari said, 'If you keep this child here, the whole of Lanka will be set on fire. The kingdom of Padmaksha was annihilated on account of this child, and the poor king was killed by the kings and demi gods who had gone there to marry her I, therefore, propose that the box should be thrown somewhere else.' Ravana was alarmed, and ordered his minister to bury the box in the kingdom of Janak, who was the bitterest enemy of the demon-king. The minister accordingly ordered his men to carry the box and bury it as directed by Ravana. The men lifted up the box, when the child said, 'I shall again come here and extirpate all the demons.' Ravana got enraged and was about to kill the child, when Mandodari prevented him from doing so. The box was then car-

* Gems.

ried at night and buried in the field presented by Janak to a Brahman. One day while the Brahman was ploughing his field, he found the box and carried it to the king. The box was opened and, to the great astonishment of all, a girl of the age of five years was found in it. As soon as the king saw her, he was moved with affection, and brought her up as his daughter. One day Purusharam, having killed all the *Kshetriyas** on earth, came to the kingdom of Janak. He went into the palace with the king to take dinner ; and when he came out after dinner, he found that some one had removed the *dhanusha*† placed by him at the court of the king. He was greatly enraged and said, 'Who has taken my dhanusha ! It is so heavy that it can not be removed even by thousands of elephants.' So saying he came out of the court with the king to look for it but, to his great surprise, he saw the girl riding on it. No sooner did she behold her father than she left the dhanusha there and ran away, when Purusharam said to the king, ' My incarnation is now over. Let the dhanusha be here. I now advise you to hold a *sayawar*‡ and marry your daughter to any man who will lift up the bow and break it off.' So saying Purusharam left for his abode. Soon after, the king held a sayawar and invited to it all the kings and Rishis on earth. All attended the sayawar including Ravana, who came there without invitation. The king told the assembly that Sita would be married to any man who would lift up the dhanusha and break it off. Many kings attempted to lift it up but they all failed in their attempt. Ravana then stepped forward and loudly said with pride and vanity, ' This bow is a trifling thing to me. I shall break it off in a second. I know, ye, weak kings and Rishis, will not be able to lift it up. It is I who would lift up the dhanusha and break it off. Sita will be my

---

*Warriors. †A bow ‡ The choosing from amongst a public assembly, of a spouse by a female.

wife, and I shall be her husband.' So saying, he began to lift up the dhanusha with all his strength and force; and while he was lifting it up, it fell heavily on his breast, and consequently he panted for breath and implored others to help him, when Rama immediately removed it, at the suggestion of Viswamitra, and broke it into two pieces. Sita, who was seated all the time on the back of an elephant, put the garland in her hands round the neck of Rama, when Ravana returned to Lanka with shame and confusion. Janak informed Dasharatha of the sayawar and requested him to come to Mithila to celebrate the marriage of his son with Sita. Dasharatha, full of joy, went to Mithila with his wives, sons, and courtiers. Soon after, Rama was married to Sita, and Varmila, Maliti and Shrutakirti, the other daughters of Janak, to Lakshuman, Bharat, and Shatrughna respectively. Rama knew that Purusharam would come and fight with him on account of the dhanusha he had broken; and, therefore, he did not like to stay any longer at Mithila. But at the request of his father-in-law he stayed there for a few days more. In the meantime, Narada went to Purusharam and told him that a man called Rama had broken his dhanusha. He was greatly enraged at this news; and having come to Mithila, he kicked up a great row about the dhanusha. To foment the quarrel Narada told him that Rama had broken the bow and that he was so proud that he did not even come down to receive him. Purusharam got indignant and let off arrows at Rama, which melted away, as soon as the latter saw them. Purusharam, knowing that his incarnation was over, laid down his arms and weapons, when Rama came down and embraced him heartily."

Soon after, Dasharatha, accompanied by his wives and ons, returned to Ayodya with exultation and joy. The ing had invited to the marriage of Rama his brother-in-aw Sangramajit, who requested the former to send Bharat and Shatrughana to spend a few days with him. Dasharatha bade his sons go with him, though they were unwilling to part with his brothers, Rama and Lakshuman for a single moment. Kayakayi pressed her sons to go with her brother; and they accordingly went with him. Rama and Lakshuman were very obedient to their parents and served them with all their heart and soul. One day the king looking to his old age, made up his mind to install Rama in the throne of Ayodya. He made every preparation to perform the ceremony of installation and invited to it all the kings and Rishis on earth. All the gods and Brahmans were afraid that if Rama was installed in the throne of Ayodya, he would not go to Lanka and relieve them from the oppression of the demons. Viranchi, one of the gods, therefore, sent one Vikalpa to go to Ayodya and prejudice Kayakayi and all the subjects of the king against Rama and put an obstacle in the performance of the ceremony, so that the prince might go to the forest of the demons and kill them all. Vikalpa tried his utmost to prejudice them against Rama; but they were all so good and pious that they remained faithful to the prince. There was only one wicked woman, Mantra, a favourite maid-servant of Kayakayi, whom he prejudiced against Rama. She hated the prince; and with a view to deprive him of the throne of Ayodya, she went into the room of Kayakayi and, throwing herself on the ground, began to beat her breast with tears in her eyes, when Kayakayi asked her what the cause of her grief was. Mantra replied, "You, unfortunate woman! Your husband is going to install Rama in the throne of Ayodya, and as soon as he is placed on the throne, he will kill your both the sons. I shall be very glad, if your Bharat is installed in the throne." Kayakayi said, "I have no objection to the installation of Rama whom I love as my son, Bharat." Mantra got exceedingl enraged and began to cry violently. Kayakayi went to quit her when Vikalpa also prejudiced her against Rama. Mantra, seeing a sudden change in her mistress, was mightily pleased with her and kissed her. Kayakayi said, "My dearest, just tell me what I should do to get rid of Rama." "Any how," replied Mantra, "we must send him away and have our Bharat placed on the throne of Ayodya. I, therefore, tell you with pleasure that if the king come to see you, ask him to fulfil the promise given by him to you during the battle he had fought with the demons in heaven. Do you remember the promise given by him to you? He promised you that he would give you whatever you would ask from him as a reward for helping him in the battle. You should, therefore, ask the king to send Rama to the forest of the demons for fourteen years and place Bharat on the throne of Ayodya. And another thing is that if the prince goes to the forest, the king will soon die of grief for his son; and it will be then a very good thing for you and your sons to pass your days in happiness." Kayakayi liked the advice of Mantra; and before the king came into her room at night, she had taken off her ornaments and thrown herself on the ground with her hair in disorder. In the meantime, the king entered her room and asked her what the matter was, when she replied, "Thou, wicked king. Be gone. I know your heart. You are going to banish my sons to a forest and give the kingdom to Rama." Dasharatha replied, "What you say is untrue, because I love Bharat and Shatrughana as much as I love Rama and Lakshuman." Kayakayi replied, "Be gone. I do not want you in my room." The king felt it bad, when Kayakayi spoke those words; and in order to pacify her he asked her what she wanted from him, when Kayakayi replied, "The promise given to me by you during the battle with the demons, must be now fulfilled. What I want from you is that you should banish Rama to the forest of the demons for fourteen years and install my son Bharat in the throne of Ayodya." The king was thunder-struck, when Kayakayi made the cruel demand, and persuaded her much to ask him for something else; but she would not mind him. In the meantime, his faithful minister, Sumant, came and informed the king, who was lying on the ground in disorder, that everything was ready for performing the ceremony of installation, when the latter told the former what had happened in the room of Kayakayi. The minister, being exceedingly sorry, went and called Rama in the room of Kayakayi. The prince came and implored his father to tell him the cause of his grief, when Kayakayi replied "The king had given me a promise at the battle with the demons that he would give me whatever I would ask from him. I have asked him to fulfil that promise, and since then he has been very sorry." Rama said, "I think, he is not able enough to comply with your demand." Kayakayi repled, " I should think so." Well" said Rama, " if my father cannot give you what you want from him, I promise to give it to you." Kayakayi replied, "Then go to the forest of the demons for fourteen years with Lakshuman and let my son, Bharat, rule in Ayodya." Rama said, " Most willingly. I have no objection to do so. It is just the same thing to me, because Bharat and I are one." Rama then, taking his leave of Kayakayi went to his mother, Kausalya, and told her what had happened. Kausalya became very sorry and said, " Thou shalt not leave me. Hide thyself in my room for fourteen years, and I shall keep the secrecy. I cannot remain without thee." Rama replied, "Mother, excuse me. I am now bound by my promise to go to the forest." So saying he threw himself at her feet and obtained her permission to go to the forest." He then went to Lakshuman and told him all that had taken place, when the latter said, "I shall accompany you. I cannot live here without you, and if you leave me here alone and go to the forest, I shall commit suicide." Rama, having consented to take Lakshuman with him, went to his wife, Sita, and said, "I am going to the forest of the demons for fourteen years; and until I return to Ayodya, I ask you to live with Kausalya. I cannot take you with me in the forest, as you are delicate and will not be able to bear hardship with me." "I shall follow you," replied Sita, "and share any misfortune that may befall you. I, therefore, go down on my knees and implore you not to leave me here alone." Whereupon Rama consulted Vashista and promised Sita that he would also take her with him. Lastly he went to take his leave of Dasharatha, when the king said with tears in his eyes, "I feel much for thee. The wicked and wretched woman has done this all, and I do not think that I shall live until thou returnest to Ayodya. I shall die of grief for thee. As I cannot tell thee to break the promise given by thee to Kayakayi, I give thee my consent to go to the forest. Child, take with thee all necessary things and pass thy days in happiness." "Father," replied Rama, "I do not want any thing. I shall dress myself in *valkalyas** and pass my days in meditation." As soon as Rama spoke these words, Kayakayi brought valkalyas and placed them before Rama, Sita and Lakshuman, who dressed themselves in them and set out for the forest with the minister, Sumant. They arrived at Shramga Vera, where Rama sat down for rest on the grass under the shade of a tree near a beautiful river and, having refreshed himself there, requested a fisherman called Guhaka, who was his devotee, to convey him with Sita and Lakshuman to the other side of the river. Guhaka asked him who he was, when he informed him that he was Rama, the eldest son of Dasharatha. Whereupon the fisherman, having embraced him, conveyed him with Sita and Lakshuman to the other side of the river, when Sumant took his leave of the prince and returned to Ayodya. Rama then went to the

* Barks of a tree.

abode of Bharadwaj, a Rishi, who worshipped him and requested him to stay with him for about fifteen days, when the prince said, "I cannot stay with you any longer, because the people of Ayodya will often come here and entreat me to return to the kingdom. I shall, therefore, go to the *Dandakaranya*."* At the request of Rama Bharadwaj showed him the way that led to the hills called Chitrakuta, where many learned Rishis lived. He went up to the hills and saw Valmika, a Rishi, and worshipped him with respect and reverence. Lakshuman built a *parnakutika*† there, and they all lived in it.

On the return of Sumant to Ayodya Dasharatha died of grief for Rama. It was a pity that none of his sons was present at the time of his death. His wives, Kausalya and Sumitra, much mourned for the king but Kayakayi did not shed a tear for him. To perform the funeral ceremony of the king his sons, Bharat and Shatrughana, were sent for, and until they returned to Ayodya, his body was preserved in a *Kadayi*,‡ full of oil. Soon after, Bharat and Shatrughana returned to the city; and, having seen the lifeless body of their father, they violently cried and much lamented for him. Vashishta said, "The body of the king cannot be burnt, unless some one is placed on the throne of Ayodya. Rama and Lakshuman have gone to the forest, and I, therefore, ask Bharat to occupy the throne, as Kayakayi has got them banished to the forest to secure the throne for him." At this information Bharat was startled, and said to Vashishta with tears in his eyes, "O! how can I bear this grief? I do not want the kingdom. I want nothing from this city. I go down on my knees and beseech you not to install me in the throne, as my beloved Rama is a rightful claimant of it. I will go wherever Rama is, and pass my days with him." Having known the

* A forest called Dandakaranya. † A small hut. ‡ A large vessel made of iron.

heart of Bharat Vashishta placed the *padukas** of Rama on the throne and proclaimed him as the king of Ayodya. Shortly after, the body of Dasharatha was carried to the funeral ground, and burnt with all his wives, except Kausalya, Sumitra and Kayakayi. Kausalya and Sumitra were ready to burn themselves with their husband, but Vashishta prevented them from doing so, as they had sons. After the funeral ceremony of Dasharatha was over, Bharat went and saw his mother, Kayakayi, when she said, "Son! I have caused Rama and Lakshuman to be banished to a forest and secured the kingdom for you with the greatest difficulty. Now without delay take charge of the kingdom, and you will be very happy. We have now no enemies; and it is a very good sign that the king has also died." Bharat got very much enraged at what he had heard from Kayakayi and replied, "You are a murderess of your husband and an enemy of Rama. It is most sinful, wicked and disgraceful on your part to cause the death of my father and the banishment of my dear brother to the forest. Rama is the rightful claimant of the throne, let him come and take his kingdom. I want nothing except Rama and shall pass my days with him in the forest." So saying he dressed himself in valkalyas and set out for Chitrakuta to join his brothers. He was followed by Vashista, Kausalya, Sumitra, Shatrughana, Sumant, and all the people of Ayodya, who were very anxious to see Rama. Thay all arrived at the river, where, Guhaka had his hut; and at the request of Bharat the fisherman conveyed all the people to the other side of the river. Lakshuman having seen the people, thought that Kayakayi had sent them to kill Rama and began to let off arrows at them. But Rama stopped him, saying that they were not his enemies. Shortly after, they all reached the paranakutika of Rama, when the prince embraced them very affectionately and asked his mother how the

* Wooden shoes.

king was doing. Kausalya, overwhelmed with grief, could not utter a word, when Vashista broke the sad news to him. He deeply mourned for his father and remained mute for a while. Vashishta condoled with him to perform the last ceremony of his father. Whereupon he went to the river, Gaya, and performed the ceremony. Kausalya, Sumitra, Vashishta, and all the people persuaded Rama to return to Ayodya and take charge of the kingdom, when he said, " I am always true to my promise, faithful to my wife, and of a firm resolution. I cannot, therefore, break the promise given by me to my mother, Kayakayi, in fulfilment of the promise given by my father to her and return to Ayodya under any circumstances." Bharat said, " If you do not come to Ayodya, I will go somewhere else and pass my days there until you return to the city." Rama stroking his head, replied, "Bharat do not be disheartened. I shall return to Ayodya in fourteen years and fourteen days. I, therefore, wish you to go back to the city and rule there on my behalf.'' Bharat said, " I am very glad to obey you, but I shall not feel there well without your company. I therefore, beg that you will kindly let me go to Nandigram and stay there for fourteen years and fourteen days." Rama replied, " If you will not be happy in Ayodya in my absence, I shall let you go to Nandigram." " But " said Bharat, "if you do not return from the forest within fourteen years and fourteen days, I shall commit suicide. " Rama, having been pleased with his brotherly feelings, gave him his padukas and sent him to Nandigram where he lived as a *Jogi** for fourteen years and fourteen days. Rama also gave his padukas to Shatrughana and bade him go to Ayodya and rule there on his behalf. Shatrughana returned to Ayodya with Kausalya, Sumitra, and all the people who had accompanied him. A few days after he had left for Ayodya, the Brahmans, who lived at

* An ascetic.

See Page 26
ALVA.
ATAPI.
AGASTI.
See Page 26.
JATAYU.
RAMA.
SITA.
LAKSHUMAN.

Chitrakuta, said, " Rama, your wife is very handsome and attractive. If you stay here with us any longer, the demons will come here and devour us all. We are informed that the demons, Trishira, Khur, and Dushan, will shortly come here to carry off your Sita. We, therefore, request you to leave this place at once." Rama replied, " You need not be afraid. Let all the demons on earth come here, I shall kill them all and defend you." The Brahmans, having no faith in what Rama had said, left the hills with their wives and children. Soon after, Rama removed to the Dandakaranya ; and on his way to the forest, he killed a demon called Viradha.

Viradha was a gandharv called Tumbar. One day Kuber, having called him in his presence to sing for him, the demi-god got tipsy and went before him. Kuber got enraged at his conduct and cursed him, saying that he would be a demon and would wander in the forest for ten thousand years but that he would be released from the curse, when he would be killed by the hands of Rama. As appointed, the gandharv was killed by Rama and released from the curse.

Rama spent thirteen years with Sita and Lakshuman in visiting holy places. And during his pilgrimage he visited the abode of Atri, a Brahman, where he worshipped the three headed god, Datatraya. Thence he went and visited Agasti, a very powerful Rishi. The story of the power of the Rishi is as follows:—

" There lived three demons called Atapi, Vatapi, and Alva. They were blessed by the god, Siva, with the art of enchantment, by means of which they devoured the innocent Brahmans. Vatapi became food and Alva water. Atapi became a benefactor and invited every Brahman to partake of the food and water. The Brahman came; and as soon as he ate the food and drank the water, Atapi cried aloud the names of Vatapi and Alva.

who, having responded to the call of their brother, tore off the body of the Brahman and came out. Thus they killed every Brahman and ate his flesh. One day Agasti was invited by Atapi to partake of the food and water The Rishi complied with his invitation; and as soon as he ate the food and drank the water, Atapi cried aloud as usual the names of his brothers but to his great surprise, they did not respond to his call, as the Rishi burnt Vatapi in his stomach. Alva, who had escaped from the belly of the Rishi, and his brother, Atapi, assumed different forms and began to run away, when the Rishi cut off the head of Atapi. Alva escaped and mixed himself with the ocean, when Agasti drank off the whole ocean and killed the demon."

Rama stayed with Agasti for a month; and during his stay there he presented him with an arrow to kill Ravana. From the Dandakaranya Rama set out for Panchavati. On the road he saw a huge bird called Jatayu, who asked Rama who he was. "I belong to the solar race," replied Rama, "and am son of the king, Dasharatha. I am called Rama." "I am son of Kasha," said Jatayu, "and the name of my uncle is Suparna, and I am called Jatayu. Your father was my great friend. I helped him during the battle which he had fought with Shukra and, therefore, he called me his brother. Having embraced Jatayu, Rama proceeded on his journey and reached Panchawati, where he lived with Sita in a parnakutika built by Lakshuman. Lakshuman gathered fruits and *kandamuls** for Sita and Rama, which they ate and passed their days there. He guarded the hut every night for fear of the demons and he himself remained without food.

One day Lakshuman went near a thicket to collect fruits and kandamuls, where he saw a deadly *khadag*†

* Esculent roots. † A sword.

See Page 26.
RAMA
SITA
LAKSHUMAN
See Page 27.
LAKSHUMAN

descending from above. The weapon fell where he was standing; and it having looked sharp and powerful, he tried it on the thicket, but, to his great astonishment, the thicket was cut into two parts, and there flowed a large quantity of blood. Lakshuman was afraid that he killed some ascetic, while meditating in the thicket; and in order to satisfy himself about it he immediately went to Rama with the khadag and informed him of what had happened, when Rama said, " Brother, do not be afraid. The blood which flows through the thicket is of a demon called Shabari. This demon is the son of Surpanakha, a sister of Ravana. He was meditating in the thicket unobserved with a view to get the weapon from Siva. The god had sent the weapon for him. If the weapon had gone to the hands of the demon, he would have annihilated the whole of the universe with it. Thank God that you have got it; and I tell you to take a particular care of it." Lakshuman was glad at this information and cheerfully attended to his duties.

On the day Shabari was killed by Lakshuman, Surpanakha found in her dream that some calamity had befallen her son; and having been awakened, she, accompanied by four demonesses, immediately started for the forest to look for her son. She wandered in the forest and at last came to the thicket; and seeing the blood there she searched the whole wood and at last found that her son was cut into two pieces. As soon as she saw her son, she fainted and cried violently for him. The other four demonesses condoled with her; and immediately after, they burnt the body of Shabari and went in search of the enemy who had killed the demon. They traced Lakshuman from his foot-prints; and in order to revenge the killing of her son, Surpanakha formed herself into a beautiful damsel; and taking with her the four demonesses, who had also formed themselves into very good maid-servants, she went to Lakshuman and said, "I have travelled all over the earth in search of a husband; but I have not found a young man as beautiful as yourself. I have become mad after you, and unless you consent to marry me, I shall not live. I, therefore, implore you to take me for your wife. Do not you see how I look? Can you get elsewhere a quite young girl like me?" Lakshuman was not at all captivated with her charms, but she having much insisted upon his giving her an answer, he replied, "I have got my brother and sister-in-law. There they live in a hut. I cannot do any thing without their consent." "I shall go to your brother," said the demoness, "and get a letter from him consenting to our match." So saying she went to Panchawati with her maid-servants and said to Rama, "I like your brother from the bottom of my heart. I have made up my mind to marry him, and he has also promised me to take me for his wife subject to your approval of the match. I, therefore, pray that you will kindly pity me and give me your letter or any other sign signifying your consent to our marriage." Sita was moved with her manner of address, and requested Rama to comply with her request. Rama surveyed her from head to foot; and finding her eye-balls upside down, he knew that she was Surpanakha in the form of a human being. Rama, therefore, said, "I have no objection to give you my consent but I shall write it on your back." "How can you do it," replied she, "I feel bashful to show you my back." "It does not matter," continued Rama. "There is no one here." At last Surpanakha told Rama to write his consent on her back, which the latter wrote and sent her away. The demoness hastened to the place where Lakshuman was standing and said, "You see, your brother has consented to our marriage with much pleasure. If you like, you may go and ask him about it. I am not a liar, you know. He has given me no letter or any sign but he has simply told you to marry me." "That will not do," replied Lakshuman, "I must have a letter or sign from my brother signifying his consent to our marriage." Surpanakha, having known his mind, showed the letter written by Rama on her back. The letter stated that as soon as Lakshuman read it, he should at once cut off the nose and ears of the demoness. Lakshuman read the letter and, having seized her by her hair, flung her down and cut off her nose and ears as directed by Rama. When her nose and ears were thus cut off, she and her maid-servants assumed their original forms and fled for fear of losing their lives, screaming hideously. Listening to her yells Trishira, Khur and Dushan came to help her with fourteen thousand demons. "Look at my nose and ears," she said to them, "There live three human beings, two males and one female. The man, who called himself Lakshuman, has disfigured me at the instigation of his brother and sister-, in-law. You must now go there and cut off their heads, so that I may drink their blood and refresh myself with it." Trishira, Khur and Dushan, having thought it below their dignity to go and fight with those human beings, selected fourteen powerful demons and sent them to Panchawati with Surpanakha, but Rama cut off their heads with one arrow Surpanakha fled in alarm and informed Trishira Khur and Dushan of what had happened. Whereupon they marched against Rama with an army of demons but they were also killed by the prince with his arrow in a moment. Surpanakha fled to Lanka in consternation and, showing her nose and ears to her brother, Ravana, informed him that Trishira, Khur and Dushan had been killed by Rama with fourteen thousand demons. Ravana was greatly alarmed at the sad news and, having called upon his uncle, Maricha, said to him, "You see, Rama has killed Trishira, Khur and Dushan and disfigured Surpanakha. If this enemy is allowed to go unnoticed, he will even kill me one day or other. I have, therefore, made up my mind to carry off Sita, his wife, to Lanka and kill Rama and Lakshuman. Please, therefore, be a beautiful *haran** and frolic at the paranakutika of Rama; and when he comes with his *dhanushaban* † to kill you, run to the heart of the forest. Rama will pursue you; and as soon as he is separated from Sita, I shall carry her off to Lanka." "It is sinful to covet one's wife," replied Maricha, "and if you carry her off, you will lose your life and everything. I, therefore, advise you to change your mind and attend to your affairs." At this advice Ravana got enraged and said, "It is a bad thing to advise me that way. It is your duty to help me on such occasions. I, therefore, command you to come with me and do what I tell you to do." Whereupon Maricha accompanied Ravana to Panchawati with the greatest reluctance. On their arrival there Ravana stood behind a thicket near the abode of Rama, and his uncle, forming himself into a stag, played tricks in front of it. Sita saw the stag and said to Rama, "Dearest, look at that stag. What a beautiful creature it is. I wish I would get its skin for my waistcoat. Please take this dhanushaban and kill it for me, so that I may have its skin for my waistcoat." To comply with the wishes of his wife Rama took up his dhanushaban and aimed at the stag. The animal began to run, and Rama went after it. When he went far off from the paranakutika, Ravana who was standing behind the thicket unobserved, imitated the voice of Rama and cried out with a view to separate Lakshuman from Sita, "Lakshuman help me. Lakshuman help me. I am in distress." Sita heard this voice and said to Lakshuman in alarm, "Rama is in distress. I have just heard him cry out for help." "You need not be afraid," said Lakshuman. "None can hurt Rama. I am sure some demon has done the mischief

* A stag. † A bow and an arrow.

with some bad motive." "Is this your affection towards your brother?" exclaimed Sita. "While Rama is actually in distress, you refuse to help him. Methinks you wish your brother's death and marry me after him." At this accusation Lakshuman shed tears and, having drawn a line around the parnakutika with his dhanushaban, said to her, "I am now going to help Rama. Look at this line. I beg you not to go behind it, and if you go, you will be in distress." So saying Lakshuman left the parnakutika with his dhanushaban; and when he went far off, Ravana disguised himself as a *Fakir*,* peeped at Sita through the door of the hut and cried out in a plaintive tone, "Is there anybody in? I am a fakir here and dying of hunger. It will be a great meritorious act, if some one comes out and gives me something to eat." Sita, who was full of kindness, came out and said, "Please sit down there. Rama will be presently here; and as soon as he comes, he will attend to your wants." "I shall not live until Rama comes here. If you now give me something to eat, I shall bless you." So saying he threw himself on the ground and pretended to be worse. Sita was alarmed and left the line to give him succor, when Ravana immediately caught hold of her and said, "Do not be alarmed. I am Ravana, the king of Lanka. I am now going to take you to my kingdom. Quietly follow me." Sita rolled on the ground and violently cried, imploring him to leave her where she was. Her tears and entreaties did not move him in the least. He seated her in a chariot and set out for Lanka. Sita all the time cried aloud the name of Rama, which Jatayu heard and went to her rescuse. "Ravana," said Jatayu, "I command you to set Sita at liberty; and if you disobey me, I shall instantly kill you." "Who art thou," replied Ravana. "What thou hast to do

* An ascetic.

with this lady ? Thou fool. Go and mind thy business." Jatayu insisted and Ravana let off arrows at him. The bird cut off with his bill all the arrows of the demon-king, broke the head of his charioteer and killed his horses. Ravana alighted, when the bird pounced upon him and pulled off his hair. He was alarmed and stood there bewildered, not knowing what to do. The bird broke his chariot, when the demon-king said, " Speak the truth. Just tell me how you will die. I shall also tell you how I shall die." Jatayu, who was a simpleton, replied " If you pull off my wings, I shall die instantly." " Now just tell me," continued Jatayu, " how you will die." " If you break my toes," said Ravana, " I shall die in no time." As soon as this secret was disclosed by Jatayu, Ravana went to catch him. The bird broke one of the toes of his enemy, when the latter pulled off his wings. Jatayu, saturated with blood, fell there rolling; and the demon-king, taking Sita on his shoulders, proceeded towards Lanka. When he reached the hills, called Matang, five powerful monkeys, Sugriva, Nala, Nila, Jambuvant and Maruti, who lived there, found the ornaments thrown by Sita on the ground. Looking at the ornaments Maruti said, "Pity, some wicked demon must have been carrying off a poor woman. I shall kill the demon and rescue her." So saying he jumped in the sky but, in the meantime, Ravana entered Lanka with his prize and despatched eighteen huge demons to search and kill Rama. A few days after his return to Lanka the demon-king said to Sita, " I beseech you to marry me. I am very powerful and have made all the gods my slaves. There is not a single soul on earth who can equal me in wealth, strength and valour. If you be my wife, you will be very happy." "Thou art wicked and a villain," replied Sita. " Thou wilt soon die. I shall never be thy wife. I loathe thee. Begone, thou fool." Having heard these words of Sita, Ravana said to himself, "Sita is very much excited; and unless she becomes calm, I shall not be able to win her heart." So saying to himself he placed her in the Asoka forest and posted five crores of demonesses with his sister, Trijata, at their head to watch her there with instructions to frighten her and make her marry him at any rate. The demonesses often showed their teeth and opened their hideous mouths as if they were going to devour her, but Sita was calm and did not heed them. Trijata, who was kind, encouraged her and told her not to frighten herself.

Lakshuman joined Rama in the forest and informed him of what had passed between Sita and himself. Lakshuman wept and Rama pacified him. They then returned to panchawati ; and finding that Sita was not in the parnakutika, they were alarmed and went in search of her. They could not find her. They then went to the Rishi, Agasti, who informed them that Sita was carried off by Ravana. They returned to their abode and saw the footprints of the demon and Sita. They immediately set out in search of Sita in the forest. On the road they met Jatayu, who informed them of what had happened. "I," said Jatayu, "mustered up all my strength and courage to rescue her from the wicked demon, but as soon as he cunningly knew my secret, he pulled off my wings and left me here in a dying state." So saying Jatayu breathed his last. Rama grieved for him and performed the funeral ceremony of his death. The princes proceeded on their journey. On the road Parwati, the wife of Siva, took the form of Sita and stood before him; but he did not receive her, as he knew that she was Parwati. A little further on, a huge demon, called Kaband, stretching his arms for some eighteen *yojans** and with his head separated from his trunk, sat

* A yojan measures nine miles.

in the forest. Rama having found that he was a demon, cut off his arms and killed the monster on the spot. Kaband was the son of Kashapa, a Rishi. One day he got drunk and frightened another Rishi, Stulashira, who cursed him, saying that he would be a demon but that he would be released from the curse when Rama would kill him. As soon as he was killed by Rama, he assumed his original form and stood before him. He said that his head was separated by Indra from his body with his *vajra**, as he was performing a severe penance to enable him to take the kingdom of the god. On the road Rama killed the eighteen demons whom Ravana had sent, and came to the Pampa *sarovar*,† where Rama and and Lakshuman sat down for rest under the shade of a banian tree. From the hills, called Rishimukha, the five monkeys saw them. Sugriva was afraid and said, "I think, Vali, my brother, has sent those two warriors to kill me." So saying he was to flee, when Maruti said, " Do not be afraid. I will ascertain who those warriors are." So saying Maruti jumped upon the tree and, having plucked off the branches of it, threw them at Rama, who cut them off with his dhanushabans. Maruti then threw large stones and mountains at him but he broke them in a minute, and hurted the monkey in the air. His father, the wind, supported him, while he was falling down, and bade him worship Rama. He came down and, having thrown himself at the feet of the prince, implored his pardon, which was readily granted by him. He became a great devotee of Rama; and one day while he was shampooing the feet of the prince he said to him, "I shall be very glad to introduce you to Sugriva, brother of the king of this place, if you promise me that you will protect him." "Just tell me who that Sugriva is," replied Rama. Whereupon Maruti related the story of the life of Sugriva, which is as follows:—

* A weapon. † A river called Pampa.

"One day while Bramhadev was performing a penance, a drop of his tears fell on his hand; and it bore a king, called Raksharaj. He was a monkey. While he was going from forest to forest, he came to a river in Kayalasa, the kingdom of Siva. He bathed in the river; but immediately after, he became a very beautiful female. It was appointed by Parwati, wife of Siva, that any man, who would bathe in the river, would be a female. Indra and the sun were enamoured of the woman. By Indra she got Vali, and Sugriva by the sun. Having heard that Raksharaj became a female, Brahmadev came to the river, and prayed to Parwati to restore his son to his former form. Parwati listened to his prayer and made Raksharaj a man again. The god then created a country called Kiskinda and gave it to him. Raksharaj ruled in the country for some time and, having placed his eldest son, Vali, on the throne, proceeded to heaven. Vali and Sugriva lived together and loved each other. Vali was very powerful and invincible, as he was presented by Indra with *Vigayamala.** After some time both the brothers became mortal enemies, and Vali carried off his beautiful wife, Ramma. For fear of his brother, Sugriva made his abode on the hills called Rishimukha Parvat. They both fought together every six months." Rama bade Maruti tell Sugriva that he would kill Vali and restore his wife to him. Maruti immediately went to Sugriva and said to him, "You are in grief for your wife, so also Rama for his wife, Sita. Rama has promised to help you in recovering your wife and you will have to help him also in recovering his wife, Sita." Sugriva was glad at what Maruti had told him and set out with his army of monkeys to see Rama. On his arrival the prince cordially received Sugriva and told him all about Sita.

---

* A garland which, if put round the neck of a warrior, always gives him success in a war.

Sugriva said that yesterday he heard screams of a woman and showed the ornaments found by the monkeys to Rama. The prince identified the ornaments as belonging to his wife and shed tears, when Sugriva said, "Do not be afraid. I shall help you with my able ministers, Nala Nila and Jambuvant in recovering Sita from Ravana. Let us kill Vali first and then we shall set out in search of Sita." As soon as Sugriva spoke these words, Rama aimed his arrow, when the former stopped him and said, "Vali is my mortal enemy and will fight with us to his last gap." Whereupon Rama asked him the cause of the enmity with his brother. "Dudhumbi, son of the demon, Maishasur," continued Sugriva, "was very powerful, and oppressed the gods in heaven and the people on earth. Nobody could fight with him. At last the demon went to Yama and challenged him to fight with him. Yama said, 'I cannot fight with you. I, therefore, tell you to go to Vali at Kiskinda and he will fight with you to your satisfaction.' The demon immediately came to Kiskinda and challenged Vali to fight with him, when the latter killed the former and hurled his body in the air which fell on the hills called Rishimukha Parwat. All the Rishis on the hills were killed by the weight of the corpse, when a Rishi called Matang cursed Vali, saying that if the latter touched the hills, he would instantly die. Mayasur, son of Dudhumbi, came to avenge the death of his father but he fled to patal through a cave, when Vali gave him blows. Vali pursued him, having posted me at the mouth of it. For many months he did not return, though I was at the cave all the time watching it. During this time demi-gods entered Kiskinda and sought to take possession of it. I, therefore, placed a mountain at the mouth of the cave and drove all the demi-gods from the kingdom. Vali did not return to Kiskinda for twenty months, and from this fact all

See Page 33
JATAYU
RAMA
LAKSHUMAN.
See Page 33
KABAND
RAMA.
LAKSHUMAN
See Page 37.
SUGRIVA
VALI
RAMA

concluded that he was no more. Whereupon the people of Kiskinda proclaimed me as their king against my wishes. In the meantime, Vali returned to the cave with the head of Mayasur and, having seen the mouth of it blocked up, he was alarmed on account of me. He immediately removed the mountain and directly came to Kiskinda. As soon as he saw me on the throne, he, boiled with rage, said, 'You blocked up the mouth of the cave with a view to kill me and take my kingdom.' So saying he attacked me but with the assistance of Nala, Nila, Jambuvant and Maruti I escaped and made my abode on these hills, because he would not come here for fear of the curse." Sugriva then showed the body of Dudhumbi to Rama, who flung it at a distance with his toe. "Now do one thing," said Rama, "Just go and challenge Vali to fight with you." Sugriva accordingly went to Kiskinda and challenged him to fight with him, when Tara said to her husband, "I implore you not to meet Sugriva today. He comes to fight with you every six months but he has now come to combat with you three days after the battle you have fought with him. I think, Rama and Lakshuman have promised to help him. I, therefore, pray that you will not go to fight with Sugriva today." "That will not do," replied Vali, "I must fight with him and cut off his head. If I am killed in the fight, Angada will protect you." So saying Vali went and attacked Sugriva, when Rama killed the former with one arrow. Tara, his wife, violently cried for her husband, when Rama consoled her and advised her to marry Sugriva. At first she hesitated; but soon after, she married him. Sugriva began to rule and forgot all about Rama in his luxury. Rama sent Lakshuman to Kiskinda. Maruti said to Sugriva, "It is a bad thing that you have forgot Rama and left him alone in the forest. There stands Lakshuman at the door of your palace. Take care he will kill us all

Sugriva was alarmed and, having thrown himself at his feet with his wives and other monkeys, implored the pardon of Rama. He then came with all his monkeys to Rama to help him in recovering his wife, Sita. Rama put his ring on one of the fingers of Maruti as a mark from him. All the monkeys set out in search of Sita. On their way they came across a forest and could not proceed further, as they were bewildered there. This forest was cursed by a Rishi, called Dandaka, saying that those who entered it would remain there bewildered. The Rishi cursed the forest, because his infant son was devoured by the goddess of the forest. The infant son became a demon and devoured all the persons and creatures that went into the forest. Angada, son of Vali, killed the demon; and as soon as he was killed, he was restored to his former form. All the monkeys escaped unhurt, as they were repeating the name of Rama all the time in the forest. They left the forest and, having searched Sita at several places in vain, at last came to a very large cave. The monkeys entered the cave but they all fainted owing to suffocation. Maruti lifted them up with his tail and came out of the cave to a place where there was a beautiful garden. All the monkeys climbed up the trees in the garden, laden with fruits, but they could not get a single fruit to eat. A mare, called Suprabha, came where the monkeys were standing. Maruti asked her who had created the garden, when the mare replied, "Brahmadev was pleased with Mayasur, a demon, and, having created the cave for him, said, 'I have created this cave for you. I require you to be always in it and not to leave it under any circumstances; and if you come out of the cave, you will instantly die.' While in the cave the demon always prayed to Vishnu for the protection of the demons on earth. Indra was alarmed and implored Bramhadev to get the demon out of the cave. To get him out of the cave the god created a very beautiful damsel called Hema and sent her in the cave. The demon looked at her and was captivated with her charms. Finding that the demon was very much taken with her, she came out of the cave, and he followed her, forgetting what Bramhadev had told him. As soon as he came out of the cave, he instantly died. After the death of the demon, Hema was in the possession of the cave and garden, and soon left for the kingdom of Vishnu, placing me here in this form to watch it. Hema told me that when monkeys would come into this garden, I would be restored to my former form." Maruti said to her, "We have eaten fruits to our hearts' content and we must now leave this place as soon as possible. We cannot see the way to the cave through which we have come here. Will you, therefore, be kind enough to show it to us?" Whereupon Suprabha told all the monkeys to shut their eyes; and in a second they were all on a seashore. She was restored to her former form and, visiting Rama, went to her husband.

The monkeys were very anxious to cross the sea and go to Lanka, but they were unable to do so. However, Maruti, repeating the name of Rama, crossed the sea; but on the way he met with several accidents. The gods sent a huge woman to devour him. She opened her mouth and stood in his way. He passed through her mouth and proceeded further. In the meantime, the sea sent a mountain to block up his way. The mountain said to him, "Good creature! Why are you not going to take rest on my bosom?" At these words Maruti got enraged and pressed down the mountain. A little further on, a frightful demoness, Shihika, who was mother of Rahu and Ketu, swallowed him up; but he tore off her belly and came out. At last he arrived at upper Lanka, when the goddess of the place caught hold of his legs and knocked him down. He got up and gave her mortal blows, when she implored him to spare her life. He having granted her request, she blessed him, saying that he would be successful in his undertaking. He then came to lower Lanka, called Padalanka. Krocha, the youngest sister of Ravana, whose husband, Gargar, was killed by Indra, lived there. As soon as she was informed of his arrival there, she went with a number of demons and demonesses to catch him, when he became a small and beautiful animal. Krocha said to the demons and demonesses, "This is a very good and pretty animal. Let me have it for my breakfast. Just kill it and cook it for me." "My body," replied he, "is full of water, and if you order me to be cooked for your breakfast, you will get nothing. I, therefore, tell you to swallow me up, so that you may have a delicious taste." Krocha accordingly swallowed up Maruti, who entered her heart and pulled off her flesh. The demoness tossed about with pain. Her companions gave her medicine mixed with the dung of a hog, but the monkey was so disgusted with the dirt that he let out his tail through her nose and ears. All the demons and demonesses believed that the tail was a disease, and began to pull it out, when Maruti, having torn off her belly, came out and threw all the demons and demonesses into the sea. From lower Lanka he went again to upper Lanka; and at sunset he entered Nikumbala, a county in Lanka, where Indrajit the eldest son of Ravana, lived with his family. He went into the palace of the demon-prince and saw him with his beautiful wife, Sulochana, there. Maruti said to himself, "No doubt this is Sita, and she has fallen in love with this wicked demon." So saying to himself he was about to kill both of them but, in the meantime, she said to her husband, "Just think for a moment. Is it not a bad thing that your father has unjustly brought Sita here? If she is not restored to her husband, a great calamity will befall him." Having heard this conversation, Maruti was convinced that she was not Sita, and went to the palace of Vibhishan, the youngest brother of Ravana, where he was much pleased, because the demon was the devotee of Rama, and every thing there was clean. He also saw there an idol of Rama, which Vibhishan worshipped every day. Thence he went to the palace of Kumbhakarna, where he was in deep sleep snorting all the time. Maruti was disgusted with the sight of the heaps of bones and the flesh of human beings and animals scattered around his palace. When he failed to find Sita there and at other places, he was enraged; and, assuming an invisible form, he began to trouble the demons and demonesses of Lanka in various ways. When they carried water in their pots, he broke them with his tail. He dashed to pieces the chariots of the princes who happened to drive in the streets. One day a barber began to shave the beard of Ravana, when Maruti stood behind him in an invisible form and thrust his tail into the nose of the former. The barber was startled; and in confusion he shaved the mustaches of Ravana. Ravana got angry and slapped the barber in the face, when the monkey also gave a slap to the demon-king. Maruti pulled down the houses of the demons with his tail, while their families were asleep. One day in a minute he extinguished all the lamps in Lanka, and consequently all of a sudden were in confusion and alarm. The inhabitants of Lanka said to themselves, "Sita, whom Ravana has brought here, has created the devil to annoy and trouble us." Maruti then entered the palace of Ravana, where he and his wife, Mandodari, were fast asleep. On beholding Mandodari, Maruti thought that she was Sita and that she fell in love with the demon-king. He got much enraged, and was about to carry them where Rama was staying with Lakshuman. But, in the meantime, Mandodari was awakened in alarm and said to her husband, "I have dreamt a dream which indicates that Indragit and you will be killed, that the Asoka forest will be destroyed, and that Lanka will be burnt, because you have unjustly brought Sita here. I, therefore, implore you to restore her to her husband." "You need not be afraid of it in the least," replied Ravana. "I have posted five crores of the demons and demonesses to watch the Asoka forest and they will not allow Rama to kill us and destroy the forest." So saying Ravana despatched his servant to the Asoka forest to see whether Sita was there. Maruti accompanied the servant in an invisible form. He saw Sita sitting under the shade of a tree. The servant returned to Ravana and Maruti remained in the Asoka forest. The monkey was exceedingly glad when he found Sita, and threw before her the ring which Rama had put on his finger. She looked at the ring and asked it with tears in her eyes, "Ring? Where have you come from? How is my Rama? Is he safe?" While Sita was thus asking the ring, the demonesses came there and told her to keep quiet, saying that if she did not listen to them, they would devour her, when Maruti, with his tail, tied up all of them together and flung them down. Some of them died and some fled. He then began to sing, which was so pleasing to her ears that she was very anxious to see who that creature was. She called the creature several times but nobody responded to her call. She was disappointed, and prepared herself to commit suicide, when the monkey came and stood before her. She asked him, "Who are you? What is your name and where have you come from?" "I am a servant of Rama, and have come here in search of you," replied Maruti. "Your Rama is well and has come to Kiskinda for you. He will shortly take you from this place. You need not be afraid of me. I am not a demon. I am son of the wind, and my name is Maruti." "Besides that ring," continued Sita, "have you got any other proof from Rama that you are his servant?" Whereupon he recapitulated all the calamaties that had befallen her; and she was thereby convinced that he was her husband's servant. "I should have annihilated Lanka in a moment and taken you to Kiskinda," said Maruti, "but Rama did not order me to do so. I am very hungry. Will you, therefore, allow me to take fruits from the trees in the forest for my breakfast?" "It is not in my power to allow you to take fruits from this place," replied Sita, "and if you forcibly take them, the demons and demonesses will kill you. I however tell you to gather for your breakfast the fruits that have fallen on the ground and not to take them from the trees with your hands and feet." "I swear that I shall not take any fruits from the trees with my hands and feet," said Maruti, "I shall take the fruits which have fallen on the ground." So saying he lengthened his tail and plucked all fruits with it; and after a few minutes he destroyed the whole of the Asoka forest. The sixty crores of the demons, who were watching the forest, at once came upon him; but he tied them up with his tail and flung them down. Some died and some fled. Hearing this news Ravana sent eight thousand demons to catch the monkey but the latter tied them up with his tail and killed them all. Ravana was greatly enraged, and sent one lac of warriors whom the monkey threw into the sea with his tail. The demon-king then sent his son, Akshaya, with a large army; but he was also killed with his other sons. Immediately after, he despatched a frightful demoness, called Asali, who had the strength of ten thousand elephants. She opened her hideous mouth one yojan in length and breadth and devoured the monkey, but the latter tore her belly off and came out. At last Ravana sent his son, Indrajit, with a large army of demons. He let off his arrows at Maruti, which the latter broke off with his hands in no time. The monkey pulled off his mugut with his tail broke his chariot and killed his horse. He took up an iron bar and went killing the demons with it, when Indrajit attempted to catch him in a snare but the monkey became as small as an atom and escaped through it every time the prince put it upon him. Whereupon Indrajit made a snare with a small noose and put it upon him, when he assumed a large form and broke the snare. When the prince failed in catching him in the snare, he combated with the monkey, but the latter flung him down on the ground. The Prince was alarmed and said to himself that if he was seized by the monkey and carried to Rama, he would be cruelly treated. So saying he hid himself in a cave, when Maruti blocked up the mouth of it with a mountain. Indrajit cried and wept. Ravana, having been acquainted with this news, imploringly said to Bramhadev, "You see, Indrajit is in difficulty. If you personally go there, you will be able to insnare the monkey. I, therefore, beseech you to do the work for me." Whereupon Bramhadev went near the cave, when Indrajit hung his head down with shame and said, "Unless you catch hold of the monkey, I can not venture to come out of the cave." Whereupon Bramhadev put upon Maruti the *Bramha pasa*,* which the latter could have broken in a minute, but he allowed himself to be caught in it and carried to the court of Ravana. Indrajit went and vainly told his father that it was he who had caught the monkey. Maruti made a coil of his tail higher than the throne of Ravana and sat upon it. The demon-king indignantly asked, "Who are you and what is the name of your master?" "You are," replied Maruti, "a great rogue. Do you know who I am? I am a ser-

* A complicated snare.

KHARA
DUSHANA
KUMBHAKARNA
See Page 2
KUBER
RAVANA
TRISHIRA

vant of that prince who had saved your life at the court of Janak and cut off the nose of your sister. You are a great villain. You have carried off his wife, Sita. I am sent by my master to ascertain whether she is here. My master will shortly invade Lanka and, cutting off your ten faces, will return to Ayodya with Sita." At these words Ravana was greatly insulted and ordered the demons to cut off the tongue, nose, ears and tail of the monkey. In obedience to the order of the king all the demons brought weapons of various sorts and began to pierce him with them but nothing could be done to him, as his body was made of *vajara*.* Ravana was alarmed and did not know what to do. At last he asked the monkey by what means he would die. "I am immortal," replied Maruti, "but if you cover my tail with cloth soaked in oil and set fire to it, I shall be immediately burnt to death. Do not leave any part of my tail uncovered, and if you do so, nothing can be done to me." Whereupon Ravana ordered his servants to cover his tail with cloth. All the demons accordingly brought innumerable heaps of cloth soaked in oil and began to cover the tail of the monkey with them, but the more they covered the tail with them, the more he lengthened it; and consequently a part of it remained uncovered. All the cloth in Lanka was finished and oil exhausted. At last Ravana ordered his servants to go to the Asoka forest and get the dress of Sita, when Maruti shortened his tail and allowed it to be entirely covered. The demons then began to set fire to the tail but they failed to light it. Maruti said, "If Ravana will blow the fire himself, it will catch my tail; and I shall be immediately burnt to death" Ravana accordingly blew the fire and the tail of the monkey was lighted. Whilst he was blowing the fire, it caught his beard; and his mustaches on one side were entirely burnt.

* A diamond.

He covered his face with his handkerchief and retired to his chamber. Maruti rolled on the ground and burnt the beards and mustaches of the demons and the hairs of the demonesses with his tail in flames. He burnt many of them to death, and in a short time one-third part of Lanka was on fire. After burning Lanka the monkey went to the Asoka forest and assured Sita that her husband would take her very soon. Thence he returned to Rama at the Pampa Sarovar with her ornament as a mark from her and a letter from Bramhadev to the prince stating what the monkey had done in Lanka and that one-third of the country burnt by him had become gold. Rama and Lakshuman were very glad to read the contents of the letter and expressed their thanks to Maruti for the trouble he had taken for them. The story of how Lanka had become gold is as follows:—

" Two Brahmans, who were brothers, always quarrelled about the *dakshana** they had got from their patrons. Their father became indignant at their conduct and cursed them, saying that they would be animals, but that the god, Krishna, would release them from the curse. One brother was transformed into a *nakra*† and another into a *gajandra*.‡. The nakra lived in water and the gajandra on a mountain. One day the gajandra accidentally came to the lake in which the nakra lived; and whilst drinking the water, the latter dragged the former in the lake. A severe fighting took place between them. The nakra severely wounded the gajandra and was about to kill him, when the latter prayed to Krishna for help. The god, listening to his prayer, rode on *Garuda*§ and hastened to the lake. Finding that his devotee, the gajandra, was wounded by the nakra, Krishna killed the crocodile and released him and the elephant from

* A present in hard cash. † A crocodile. ‡ An elephant.
§ An eagle called Garuda on which Krishna always rode.

the curse. After releasing them from the curse Krishna prepared himself to return to Dwarka, when Garuda said to him, 'I am very hungry. Please, therefore, give me something to eat.' 'I shall postpone my departure for an hour or so,' replied Krishna, 'and in the meantime, you can eat the corpses of the nakra and gajandra.' Whereupon Garuda went and picked up the corpses with his bill and sat on a tree called Jambuvraksha for the purpose of eating them. But the branch of the tree on which he had sat, was broken by his weight, when he observed that millions of Rishis sat in meditation on the leaves of the branch. In order that the branch might not fall on the ground and kill the Rishis, he firmly held the branch by his bill; and not knowing where to keep it, he went to his father, Kasyapa, a Rishi, and informed him of his difficulty. Whereupon Kasyapa requested the Rishis to come down, and they complied with his request. He then told Garuda to leave the branch on a mountain at Lanka. Garuda accordingly did it and went away. The branch remained on the mountain and was converted into gold; and when Maruti burnt Lanka, it was melted by the heat of the fire and the liquid overflowed the part of Lanka which was burnt by the monkey."

Soon after, Rama and Lakshuman made preparations for march against Ravana; and on the day of *Dasara** they set out with eighteen *padmas*† of monkeys, seventy-

---

* "This festival is held on the 10th of Aswin Shud. It is called Durga Puja. On this day, in commemoration of the victory of Devi, the wife of Siva, over the buffalo-headed demon, Maheshasur,—her image, after having been worshipped for nine days is thown into the water. On this day Marathas and Kshatryas, or those who consider themselves of the military race, worship the implements of war and ask protection of them throughout the year, under a conception that to the propitiousness of the sword they owe every prosperity." † Ten billions are equal to one padma.

two *kotis** of warriors under the command of an old monkey, Jambuvant, and fifty-six kotis of other monkeys. When they arrived at the sea which Maruti had first crossed, they were encamped there, there being no way to proceed further. This news having spread throughout Lanka, Vibhishan, the youngest brother of the demon-king, entreated him to restore Sita to her husband, and set all the gods at liberty. He said, "If you do not listen to me, the whole of Lanka will be annihilated and all the demons destroyed." Ravan and his son, Indrajit, replied, "We do not care at all about it. Let Rama and all the monkeys come upon us, we shall kill them all in a second." Having failed to persuade the demon-king to restore Sita to Rama, Vibhishan, accompanied by four demons, came where the monkeys had been encamped and sought to visit the prince. The monkeys were about to kill the demons, when Vibhishan said, "I am the youngest brother of Ravana and have come here to see Rama. I hear that he killed Vali and gave his kingdom to Sugriva. In like manner, I want him to kill Ravana and give his Lanka to me. He is wicked, and has oppressed both the gods and Brahmans." The monkeys looked upon him with suspicion and did not believe at first what he had said. But Maruti said, "Vibhishan is not a wicked demon. He is a devotee of Rama, and has come here with some good object." Whereupon Rama desired the monkeys to allow Vibhishan to see him. Sugriva went and brought him to Rama. The demon fell at the feet of the prince, when the latter blessed the former saying that he would be the king of Lanka and would reign there as long as the sun and the moon last. Rama asked him what he should do to cross the sea with his large army of monkeys, when Vibhishan replied, "Pray to the sea, and he may make way for you and your army."

* One koti is equal to ten millions.

Rama went to pray to the sea and Vibhishan left for Lanka. Ravana was informed by a demon called Shardula, that a large army of monkeys under the command of Sugriva had been encamped near the shore of the sea and that they would invade Lanka in a day or two. Whereupon a demon called Shuka came to Sugriva on behalf of Ravana and said to him, "Rama is a wicked man, and why do you help him ? What have you to do with Sita ? Quietly return home with your army. If you do not listen to me, the heads of all your monkeys will be cut off ; and Rama, Lakshuman and you will be killed." The monkeys were enraged at what the demon had said and beat him severely, when Lakshuman interfered and let him go. The demon again said, "You are all stupid donkeys and will be shortly sacrificed here." Rashabha, a monkey, replied, "Just tell Ravana to restore Sita to Rama; and if he refuses to do so, his neck will be cut off with his ten heads." "Hold your tongue," said Shuka, "Sita will never be restored to Rama. I again tell you to leave the prince alone here; and if you do not listen to me, your days are numbered." The monkeys again caught him by his neck and, having belabored him, bound him with a cord.

Rama prayed to the sea for three days without eating a morsel of food; but the sea was so impertinent that he did not listen to his prayer, when the prince got indignant and aimed his dhanushaban to dry up the sea. The sea was alarmed and said, "Kindly forgive me and do not dry me up. I am ready to do what you bid me do." "Very well," replied Rama, "but what shall I do with this dhanushaban ? It must be at any rate let off according to my solemn resolution which cannot be changed under any circumstances." "There lives in the west a demon" called Maru, continued the sea. "He devours all creatures in the water. Please, therefore, let off the arrow at him and cut off his head." Rama accordingly discharged the arrow at him and cut off his head. When the head fell on the ground, it drank off a sheet of the sea-water in the west and thereby a tract of land, which is now called Marwad, was formed. The sea regarded Rama as his son-in-law and presented him with a dress and ornaments, which he accepted at the request of the monkeys; and when he wore them, he looked very beautiful. Rama asked the sea what means he should adopt to cross the water with so many monkeys, when he said, "You can have a *shetu** built over me. Let it be built by Nala with stones and mountains, which will float on the surface of the water only by his hands. When Nala was young, he always worshipped *shaligrams*† and threw them into the sea-water. A Rishi was pleased with him and blessed him, saying that by his hands, stones and mountains would float on the water." So saying to Rama, the sea disappeared. Immediately after, Rama called Nala and said to him, "To cross the sea, a shetu must be built by you of stones and mountains, which will float on the water by your hands only. I, therefore, beg you to order all the monkeys to procure stones and mountains and lay them by your hands in the water." Nala was puffed up with pride and said to himself that the shetu could not be built without him. So saying Nala ordered the monkeys to get stones and mountains which the latter brought and gave in charge of the former. Nala built a portion of the shetu, but the fishes in the sea ate it. He again built it but the fishes again ate it. He was at a loss to know what to do, when Maruti said to him, "Pride goeth before destruction. You thought that the bridge could not be built without you. What do you say now ? Leave off your pride and be humble. Now write the name of

* A bridge or pool. † A black stone found in the river Gadanki, and worshipped as sacred to Vishnu.

Rama on each stone and lay it in the water; and if you do this, you will be able to build the shetu within a short time. Nala did it as directed by Maruti; and the shetu was built one hundred yojans in length and breadth so far as Suvela without any difficulty. After the shetu was completed, Rama crossed it with his army and came to Suvela, where he encamped his army.

Rama set Shuka at liberty, who went to Ravana and informed him of what had happened to him and how they had built the shetu. He requested the demon-king to submit to the prince and restore Sita to him. Ravana got very indignant and said, "You are alarmed, because they beat you. If you advise me that way again, I shall at once cut off your head." Soon after, Ravana sent two demons, Shuka and Surna, to Suvela to ascertain the position of the army of Rama. The two demons in the forms of monkeys mixed themselves with the monkeys belonging to the army of the prince. Vibhishan informed Rama that the demons had come to Suvela in the forms of monkeys to ascertain the position of his army. Whereupon Rama ordered the monkeys to allow the demons to count their numbers. The two demons were accordingly taken round the whole army. They, having seen it, returned to Lanka and said to the demon-king, "Rama has got a large army of monkeys, and it will be very difficult for you to defeat it. We, therefore, implore you to submit to Rama and restore Sita to him." Ravana was enraged and threatened them that he would cut off their heads, if they advised him that way. He then, accompanied by the two demons, went to the top of his tower to see the army of Rama. Vibhishan came and informed the prince that the demon-king had gone to his tower to have a look at his army, and while he was there, Sugriva jumped from Suvela, which was at a distance of hundreds of miles from Lanka, and returned to his camp with the mugut of Ravan. The demon-king was alarmed, and immediately came downstairs. A few days after, he said to his courtiers, "I have now no patience. I must marry Sita as soon as possible. If any of you make her love me and marry me, I shall be ever grateful to him." Whereupon his minister, Vidynjiva, who was well versed in magic and sorcery, replied, "I shall create, by means of sorcery, a head well cut off and similar to that of Rama and also a dhanushaban and show them to Sita, so that she may be convinced that her husband has been killed. If she is convinced of it, she will become hopeless and easily love you and marry you." "I am very much thankful to you for your excellent scheme," replied Ravana. "There is no doubt you will succeed in it." Vidynjiva accordingly created the head of Rama and his dhanushaban. Ravana then came to the Asoka forest and said to Sita, "I am very sorry to inform you that your darling husband is killed and that his brother, Lakshuman, has fled to Ayodya. Maruti, Sugriva, Nala, Nila, Angada and all other warriors are also killed. You are alone here, what can you do now? You are helpless. I, therefore, beseech you to marry me. You shall be my first wife and Mandodari will be your maid-servant. Alas! Sita, Rama is no more. Believe me. If you want any proof of what I say, here is the head of your Rama cut off by a demon, and here is his dhanushaban." As soon as Sita beheld the head of Rama and his dhanushaban, she fainted. In her grief she said to Ravana. "I look upon you as my father and implore you to order a pile of wood to be arranged, so that I may set fire to it and burn myself in it. I do not wish to live any longer in this world." As soon as he heard these words, he returned to his court, leaving Sita alone there. In the mean-time, Sharma, wife of Vibhishan, came to the Asoka forest and informed her that Rama was doing well and that the head, which was shown to her, was cre-

See Page 49
SHUKA
MONKEYS
MONKEYS
MARUTI
MONKEYS
BRIDGE
RAMA
LAKSHUMAN
THE SEA
See Page 50
See Page 52
DEMONESSES.
RAVANA
SITA
HEAD OF RAMA

ated by the demons by means of sorcery to make her give up her hope of Rama and marry Ravana. No sooner did Sharma inform Sita of this than the created head and dhanushaban which were left there, disappeared. Soon after, the demon-king said to his wife, "Mandodari, you are my faithful wife and love me much. I have a great passion for Sita; and if you do not help me, I shall die. If you really love me, go to Sita in the Asoka forest and persuade her to marry me." Whereupon Mandodari went to Sita and, having communicated her husband's wishes to her, returned home. She said to her husband, "Dearest, Sita is not a woman who will comply with your wishes. She is a paragon of virtue. She will sacrifice her life rather than yield to your passion. There is no use of your being after her. I, therefore, beseech you to restore her to Rama. Why do you covet another's wife?" "My love," replied Ravana, "What you say is true, but I shall never submit to Rama and humiliate myself in the eyes of all nations. I shall fight with him and die but I shall never restore Sita to him." Having failed to persuade her husband, she returned to her palace. Ravana again went to the top of his tower with his courtiers and began to look at the army of Rama. Rama also went to the top of a hill with Sugriva and other monkeys and began to look at Ravan and his courtiers. Whilst Ravana was looking at the army of the prince, Sugriva jumped from the hill and knocked down the muguts put by him on his ten heads. The demon-king was surprised and combated with the monkey but the latter, having administered to him severe blows, returned to Rama with joy. Ravana was alarmed, and immediately came down with shame and confusion. After all preparations for the war were completed on both the sides, Vibhishan said to Rama, "Before an attack is made on Ravana, it is advisable to negotiate with him for peace. You should, therefore, send an ambassador to his court and request him to restore Sita to you." Rama accordingly sent Angada to the court of Ravana but no-body noticed him there. The monkey was, therefore, irritated and said to the demon-king, "Ravana, do you know who I am?" "Who are you and what is your name," Ravana indignantly asked. "I am a servant of Rama," continued Angada, "and my name is Angada. I am son of Vali. I have come here to negotiate with you for peace." "I shall never make peace with Rama," replied Ravana. "I tell you once more to make peace with Rama," said Angada, "and restore Sita to him. If you refuse to listen to me, you will lose your life and every thing in Lanka. He is very powerful, and you can do nothing to him." "You are a shameless creature," Ravana indignantly replied, "You know very well that Rama has killed your father and, instead of revenging yourself upon the enemy you have now come to help him. You are a great donkey." "No doubt, Rama killed my father," said Angada, "but by his arrow he has gone to heaven where he now enjoys ever-lasting happiness." Ravana was furious, and ordered four demons to bind Angada. Whereupon the demons firmly held him by his arms, when the monkey struck the chest of Ravana with his tail and jumped from Lanka with his muguts, chatra and *mandap** and returned to Suvela. The four demons, with whom the monkey had jumped, hung upon his shoulders with their heads downwards, and were killed by a fall on the ground.

The negotiations for peace having fallen through, Susen marched against Lanka with twenty kotis of monkey-soldiers and fought with the troops of Ravana under the command of Dhamaraksha. Susen routed and defeated them all, and their commander was killed by Maruti with blows. The news of the defeat having spread through-

* A pavilion.

out Lanka, the demon-king, boiled with rage, sent the demons, called Vazra Dausti and Sukpana, with a number of demon-soldiers, but they were also defeated with heavy loss. Ravana was alarmed and did not know what to do. But, in the mean-time, his son, Indrajit, kept the field with the warriors, Janbumali and Vidyaman and let off arrows at the army of Rama which the latter cut off and killed the two warriors. Whereupon Indrajit immediately jumped with his chariot into the sky, where he hid himself in the clouds and let off serpent-weapons at the army of Rama, which produced innumerable serpents. These serpents stung Rama and Lakshuman and all their soldiers; and consequently they all fell lifeless in the field, except Maruti and Vibhishan, who were immortal. Indrajit, having thus defeated Rama, returned to Lanka with a great success. The demon-king was very glad at the success of his son and said to his sister, Trijata, " Sister ? Look at the valor of our Indrajit. How has he fought and how has he defeated the army of Rama ? You know, nobody on earth can conquer us. Now what I want you to do is that you should now go to Sita and inform her of all that had happened. Show her Rama, Lakshuman and their soldiers lying lifeless in the field and tell her that she is now helpless and I am the only one who can support her. Tell her all this and persuade her to marry me. O ! sister, I like her much." Trijata accordingly showed to Sita, Rama, Lakshuman and the monkey soldiers lying lifeless in the field and told her all that Ravana had said. Sita, having seen her beloved Rama and Lakshuman, violently cried and became hopeless. Maruti and Vibhishan consulted together as to what they should do to resusitate the princes and their army, but before they arrived at a certain conclusion, the wind had come and whispered to Rama a garuda mantra which produced garudas or eagles. These garudas killed all the serpents and resusitated Rama, Lakshuman and their army. The fighting was again renewed by the monkeys, when Pravasta, the minister of Ravana, bravely fought with them and killed many of them. Whereupon Nala threw at the minister one lac of mountains which the latter broke in no time and continued the fighting. But after a hot battle Pravasta was killed by Nala with a tree called Tada, a hundred yojans in length. At this defeat, Ravana was greatly enraged and prepared himself to fight with the enemies, when his wife, Mandodari, said to him, " My dearest, you should now give up the idea of your fighting with Rama any longer. Why do you want another's wife ? My love, just restore her to her husband, so that every thing may end in peace and tranquillity." " My darling," Ravana laughingly replied, " I am ready to do any thing for you but please do not tell me to restore Sita to Rama. I am prepared to fight with him and kill him with all his army." Ravana having refused to listen to her, she returned to her palace. Immediately after, the demon-king kept the field with his sons, grand-sons, great grand-sons and a large number of warriors and soldiers and commenced operations, when Sugriva threw a large mountain at him, which the latter broke with his arrows. Whereupon all the monkeys rushed upon him with mountains, large trees, rocks and other weapons but he also broke them with his arrows. Maruti then threw a very large rock at the demon-king which the latter broke with his arrows and gave blows to the former. Maruti fainted for some time and, having soon come to himself, returned the blows to him and knocked down his muguts and the chatras held over his ten heads. Ravana was not in the least alarmed and continued the fighting. Whereupon Nala produced by a mantra innumerable Nalas like himself and employed them to throw mountains,

See Page 55
INDRAJIT
VIDHISHAN
MONKEYS
LAKSHUMAN.
RAMA
See Page 57
KUMBHAKARNA
MONKEYS.

trees and rocks at the demon-king, when the latter let off a *Bramhasra** and made them all disappear in a second. Lakshuman then let off a *Bramhaskti** at Ravana, which was cut off by the latter into two parts. One part of it fell on the ground and with another Lakshuman was struck; and consequently he fainted. Maruti was greatly enraged and gave Ravana blows, which made him vomit blood and return to Lanka. When the demon-king was thus defeated, he sent his demon-subjects to arouse his brother, Kumbhakarna, from his fast sleep. The demons went and shook him but he was not awakened. Whereupon they threw rocks and mountains at him, pierced him with sharp weapons, and scratched him with their nails, but nothing could arouse him from his sleep. He was snorting with a great noise and drew in and sent out with his inspiration and respiration the demons, bullocks, cows, elephants and other animals that had come before him. At last the demons brought two nymphs and made them sing before him. By their melodious voice he was aroused; and as he was hungry for six months, he at once devoured billions of bullocks, she-buffaloes, Brahmans, cows and even demons, and drank off gallons of liquor and *ghee*†. After his hunger was appeased, the demons informed him of what had happened to his brother, Ravana, his kingdom and subjects. Whereupon Kumbhakarna immediately stood on his legs and began to walk towards the palace of his brother. The monkeys, looking at the huge size of the demon, were greatly disheartened but Maruti went to him and lifted him up thrice in order that they might not be afraid of him. Kumbhakarna reached the palace of Ravana and stood before him, when the latter said to him, " Brother ? I am now in difficulty. I have brought Sita, the wife of Rama, as I wish to marry her. In order to recover her from me Rama has

---

* A weapon. † Clarified butter.

come here with a great number of monkey-soldiers. They have killed good many demons and destroyed nearly the whole of Lanka. It is now your duty to help me." "It is not good that you have deprived the helpless woman, Sita, of her husband," replied Kumbhakarna. "It is a great sin that one should covet another's wife. You ought to have restored her to her husband. But as you have brought her here at the risk of your life, have you fulfilled your wishes? If not, transform yourself into Rama and go to her." "That cannot be done," replied Ravana, "because if I become Rama, all his virtues will reign in me and prevent me from doing any wicked act. Unless you kill Rama, I shall not be able to fulfill my wishes." "As you are my brother," said Kumbhakarna, "it is my duty to help you. Have courage. I shall devour all the monkeys in a moment and kill Rama and Lakshuman." Taking his leave of Ravana, Kumbhakarna attacked the army of Rama, when four monkeys, including Sharab and Govaksha flung mountains and rocks at the demon which the latter broke with blows and threw them into the sky. Kumbhakarna devoured a great number of the monkeys but a few of them escaped through his ears and nostrils. Sugriva then threw a mountain at him which the latter broke with one blow and, having held him by his feet, turned him round like a reel. He was about to dash the monkey to pieces, when the latter escaped from his clutches and jumped into the sky. But he, having stretched out his hands in the sky, brought him down and put him into his arms. Sugriva was disgusted at the stink of his arms and, having cut off his nose and ears, once more escaped and jumped into the sky of which Kumbhakarna knew nothing. He was profusely bled and altogether disfigured. Having thought that he was successful in the war, he walked towards the palace of his brother, Ravana.

The demon-king was ashamed to behold him in that state; and in order to avoid an interview with him he ordered his barber to show him a mirror. The barber accordingly held a mirror before the demon in which he beheld his disfigured face and immediately returned in a great rage to renew the fight with the monkeys. Desperate as he was, he devoured many of the monkeys and attempted to rush upon Rama, when Lakshuman let off arrows at him, which he broke with his hands. In the mean-time, Vibhishan went to fight with his brother, when the latter said, "You are a great scoundrel. Do you know who I am? I am your brother. You are treacherous, and have joined our enemies. I should have just killed you on this spot, but as there will be no one left behind us to perform our funeral ceremonies, I spare your life and command you to leave this place immediately. Do not show me your face again." Having heard these words from the mouth of Kumbhakarna, Vibhishan immediately disappeared. Kumbhakarna then rushed upon Rama, when the latter let off arrows at him, but they all were devoured by the demon. Lastly the prince discharged a deadly arrow at him and cut off his hands with it, and, with other arrows, his feet, trunk, and head. On receiving the news of the fall of Kumbhakarna in the field Ravana much grieved for him, when Indrajit came and consoled his father. Immediately after, Atikaya, the second son of Ravana, with other warriors, abravely attacked the army of Rama and shot a great number of the monkeys; but at last Lakshuman killed him with his arrow. Ravana much lamented for him, when Indrajit consoled his father and, having washed his body with the blood of human beings and cows, performed a penance. His goddess was pleased with him and presented him with a chariot, horses and weapons. He seated himself in that chariot and jumped into the sky; and having hid himself in the clouds, he let off arrows at the monkeys and killed them all. Even Rama and Lakshuman were struck with his arrows. The demon-prince again returned to Lanka with success. To resuscitate the monkeys, Maruti went to get a mountain called Dronagiri, which was full of medicinal plants. For some time he stood at the foot of the mountain entreating him to accompany him to Suvela, the place of the war, and resuscitate the monkeys with his medicinal plants. The mountain said "Be gone. You, fool. I am not expected to accompany you to Suvela. Depart from this place." Maruti got indignant at the insolence of the mountain and, having lifted him up with his tail, brought him to Suvela. By the odour of the medicinal plants on the mountain all the monkeys with Rama and Lakshuman were resuscitated; and soon after, they entered Lanka and set fire to it. Whereupon Ravana sent the demons, Jang Prachang, Krochen, Nikumbha and others to oppose them and quench the fire. The demons let off a rain-weapon, which produced water and quenched the fire. By his mantra Indrajit then created a female called Kritya and jumped with her into the sky; and hiding himself behind her back he let off arrows at the monkeys and killed many of them, when Rama, at the suggestion of the wind, let off the weapon called Angirastra, which cut off the female. Whereupon Indrajit immediately came down and, having defeated the army of Rama with heavy loss, returned to Lanka with success. The monkeys were alarmed, when Maruti immediately kept the field. At this time Indrajit created by his mantras a woman exactly like Sita and, having seated her in his chariot, came to the field and loudly said in the hearing of all the monkeys, "You see, on account of this wretched woman my father has suffered much. If her head is cut off, every thing will end in peace, and there will be no war" So saying he cut off the head of the woman and immediately went to his county, Nikumbala, to perform a penance with a view to get from the deity of fire a *divyaratha** with horses and weapons. He entered a solitary place and, posting demons to watch it, began to perform the penance. Indrajit killed for the purpose many Brahmans and cows and, washing his body with their blood, seated himself upon corpses and carcasses, made a *havan*† and offered the deity of fire the heads of Brahmans and cows. The deity having been pleased with him, half of the divyaratha came out of the havan.

Maruti believed that the woman, whose head had been cut off, was Sita and communicated the sad news to Rama and Lakshuman, which disheartened and disappointed all. In the meantime, Vibhishan came and informed Rama and the monkeys that Sita was safe in the Asoka forest and that the Sita, whose head was cut off by Indrajit, was created by him with his mantras. He also informed them of the penance and said, "Half of the divyaratha has come out of the fire; and if the whole chariot come out, you will not be able to conquer Indrajit. I, therefore, advise you to go to Nikumbala as soon as possible and destroy the havan, so that the chariot may disappear and not come to the hands of the demon-prince. I also tell you that as soon as you destroy the havan, he will be desperate and fight with you; but no one will be able to kill him, unless he has observed fast for 12 years." Listening to what Vibhishan had said Rama made a sign to Lakshuman, who had observed fast for 14 years, and bade him go with Maruti, Sugriva, and the other monkeys to Nikumbala to destroy the havan and kill Indrajit. Lakshuman accordingly went with them to Nikumbala and destroyed the chariot and havan. The noise of the monkeys aroused Indrajit who was in deep meditation; and find-

* A beautiful, fine and charming chariot. † Oblation by fire to a deity.

ing that the havan was destroyed, he was so furious that he let off at them a rain-weapon, which produced the rain and flowed the army of Lakshuman. The prince discharged a wind-weapon, which produced the wind and dispersed the rain. Indrajit stopped the wind by a mountain-weapon, which produced innumerable mountains, when Lakshuman let off a diamond-weapon, which produced diamonds, and broke the mountains. Indrajit let off a fire-weapon, which produced fire and began to burn the army of Lakshuman, when the latter discharged a sea-weapon, which produced volumes of water and extinguished the fire. Indrajit lastly let off five arrows and struck Lakshuman with them, when Vibhishan threw his *gada** at the demon-prince, who cut it off and struck his uncle with five arrows. At last Lakshuman let off a deadly arrow and broke his head with it, and his chariot was broken and horses killed by Jambuvant. Indrajit however fought alone on the ground, when all the monkeys threw at him innumerable mountains, rocks, and trees at one and the same time, but he broke them with his arrows in no time. He then jumped into the sky and, hiding himself in the clouds, let off arrows at Lakshuman when Maruti placed the latter on the palm of his hand and lifted him up in the sky, where he fought with Indrajit. Whereupon the demon-prince came down, when Maruti brought Lakshuman on the ground. They fought for some time on the ground but at last Lakshuman cut off with his arrows the thighs, arms and the head of his enemy. One of the arms of the demon-prince, when cut off, fell down in the compound of the palace of his wife, Sulochana, a daughter of Shesha, and the monkeys carried off the head to their camp with exultation. Rama rejoiced at the success and told the monkeys to preserve the head and hand it over to a woman, who would come hither to ask for it. Sulochana came out of her room, and as soon as

See Page 59.
KUMBHAKARNA.
BARBER.
See Page 59.
INDRAJIT
See Page 62.
LAKSHUMAN
INDRAJIT
MARUTI

she identified her husband's arm, she took it up in her hands and lamented over it. She said to the arm with tears in her eyes, "My love, just let me know how you were killed. If I am faithful to you, let this your arm write a short account of the battle you had fought with Rama." So saying she placed a piece of paper, pen and inkstand before the arm, which wrote the full account of the battle and informed her that the monkeys carried off his head to Suvela. As soon as Sulochana read the account, she grieved much and placed the arm and paper before his father-in-law, Ravana. Ravana read the letter and fainted away, when Mandodari came out of her room and, hearing the sad news of the fall of her brave son, violently cried and wept. Sulochana said, "I am going to burn myself with my beloved Indrajit. I, therefore, implore you to get his head back from the monkeys." At the entreaties of his daughter-in-law the demon-king was moved, and pitied her; and at the same time, he was boiled with rage at the monkeys, and exclaimed, "Daughter, I shall get the head back. Rest assured. I will now fight with Rama and never return, unless I kill him." So exclaiming he ordered his courtiers to make prepartions for march against the prince, when Mandodari said to Sulochana, "There is no necessity for fighting with Rama. If you go to him alone, he will give the head to you, as he is very kind." Ravana said, "She is helpless, if any body commit outrage upon her." "There is not a single monkey with Rama," replied Mandodari, "who will covet another's wife." As soon as Mandodari said these words, he hid his face with shame and confusion and allowed Sulochana to go alone to Suvela. Sulochana came to the camp of the monkeys, when the latter took her to Rama. She said to the prince, "I am wife of Indrajit and have come hither to carry the head of my husband, as I am going to burn myself with him. I, therefore, implore you to give it to me." "How did you know that the head of your husband was carried off by us," asked the monkeys. Sulochana told them what had happened but the monkeys said to her, "We can not believe what you say. It is impossible that a lifeless arm can write. Here is the head of your husband; and if you were faithful to him, just make it laugh; and then we will be convinced of what you say." Whereupon Sulochana, embracing the head, said, "My love, I am now in difficulty. These monkeys have met here together to judge of my fidelity towards you; and if your head does not laugh, they will look upon me as a vile woman." Sulochana tried her utmost to make the head laugh but it did not listen to her. At last she said, "I made a great mistake. If I had called my father, Shesha, to help you, nothing could have been done to you." As soon as she uttered these words, the head heartily laughed. The monkeys said, "Though Sulochana spoke to the head in so many pathetic words, it did not laugh but as soon as she took the name of Shesha, it heartily laughed." "What is this mystery?" asked the monkeys. "Sulochana is the daughter of Shesha," replied Rama, "and Lakshuman is an incarnation of Shesha. The head laughed, because his father-in-law killed his own son-in-law." No sooner did Rama inform the monkeys of this than Lakshuman much grieved for his son-in-law, Indrajit, when the former pacified and consoled him, saying that he would resuscitate the demon-prince, if he wished him to do so. But at the entreaties of the monkeys Rama did not resuscitate Indrajit. The monkeys then handed the head over to Sulochana, which she took and brought on the seashore near Lanka, where she arranged a pile of wood and, having set fire to it, burnt herself with the head. Ravana, who was present there with his family according to the custom, was deeply affected at the sight, and returned home over-whelmed with grief. Ravana was in a confused state of mind, and did not know what to do, when his minister, Vidya, advised him to write a letter to his uncles, Ahiravana and Mahiravana, in Patal. Whereupon the demon-king wrote to them, called them to see him at his palace and informed them of his misfortune and distress, when they encouraged him and said, "You need not be alarmed. We shall carry off Rama and Lakshuman to Patal today at midnight and sacrifice them to our goddess." The ministers of Vibhishan overheard what had passed between Ravana and the demons and communicated it to their master. Whereupon Vibhishan told Maruti, Nala, Nila, Sugriva and other monkeys to guard Rama and Lakshuman during the night. All the monkeys, therefore, made a fortification of their tails and, placing in it the princes on a cot, guarded them. At midnight Ahiravana and Mahiravana came there and were greatly surprised at the curious fortification. But there being no way to get in, they excavated the earth; and through that excavation they carried off the princes with the cot to Mahikavati in Patal, where they put them in trance and confined them in a house. They had posted twenty kotis of demons under the command of Makardwaja to watch the mouth of the excavation which was near the sea in Patal.

At the dawn of the day all the monkeys at Suvela went to visit Rama, when they found, to their great surprise, that the cot disappeared with Rama and Lakshuman. They saw the excavation and the footprints of the demons, from which they concluded that the demons had carried off the princes through that hollow. All the monkeys were greatly alarmed, and did not know what to do, but, in the mean time, Vibhishan came and told them not to make a noise about it, because if Ravana knew of their position, he would attack them and kill them all in no time. The monkeys with Vibhishan met together and asked Maruti whether he could go through the excavation and trace the whereabouts of Rama and Lakshuman. "Even at the risk of my life I will get Rama and Lakshuman back," replied Maruti. Having thus spoken Maruti entered the excavation with Nala, Nila, Angada, and Jambuvant and went through it to the sea-shore half dead, where they refreshed themselves with a fresh breeze. Looking at the large numbers of the demons they disguised themselves as *Fakirs** and asked the monsters to show them the way that led to Mahikavatî. The demons did non listen to them and prevented them from proceeding further, when Maruti got indignant and threw them into the sea with his tail. Makardwaja was greatly incensed, and combated with Maruti but the latter flung him down and sat on his chest. Makardwaja was alarmed, when Maruti called upon him to name the espouser of his cause. "If my father, Maruti, were here," said Makardwaja, "he would kill you and save my life." As soon as the demon mentioned the name of Marutî, the latter wa startled, and, getting up from his chest, said, "My name is Maruti. I am a *Bramhacharî* † and how do you say that I am your father? Just give me an account of how you were born to me." "When you burnt Lanka," replied Makardwaja, "you threw into the sea your sweat, which my mother, a *Magarî*, ‡ swallowed up; and of that sweat I was born to you." Maruti was astonished at the account given by Makardwaja, and blessed him when, the Magari came to see the monkey and said to him, "When you came here last time, you had a large size; but I now find that your form is very small. I doubt whether you are that Maruti whom I had seen." Whereupon Maruti assumed his former form and removed her doubt. He then acquainted her with what had happened

* Mendicants. † A Brahman that religiously abstains from all sexual commerce with woman; either for a time or through life. ‡ An alligator.

to Rama, when she said, "Ahiravana and Mahiravana are two brothers. They are wicked and treacherous demons. I know that they have carried off Rama and Lakshuman to Mahikavati, and they will sacrifice them to their goddess tomorrow. I, therefore, advise you to go and hide yourself in the temple of the goddess, where you will find both the princes." "Have patience," replied Maruti, "I will kill all the demons and give Mahikavati to your son." "Mahikavati," continued the Magari, "is at a distance of 13 yojans, and to reach there you will have to cross a vast sea, which you will not be able to do. I, therefore, beg you to sit with your companions in my mouth, and I will convey you to that place." Nala, Nila, Angad, and Jambuvant were afraid, as they thought that the Magari might swallow them up on their way to Mahikavati. They, therefore, refused her kind offer and stayed on the sea-shore, while Maruti alone jumped over the sea and immediately reached Mahikavati, where he became as small as an atom and entered the temple of the goddess. As soon as he saw the goddess, he put her into a drain and, assuming her form, sat in her place. The goddess was frightened, and did not speak a word for fear of life. The demons as usual made offerings to the goddess consisting of boiled rice, milk, butter and other things which Maruti swallowed up to his heart's content and loudly said to the demons, "I am very much pleased with you, because you have brought today Rama and Lakshuman for my tiffin Let me have them. Do not open the doors of the temple, because you will not be able to bear my power and lustre. I, therefore, command you to make an opening to one of the walls of the temple and push them in through it, so that I may devour them with a great relish. Do not kill them." Believing that the goddess was much pleased with them, Ahiravana and Mahiravana removed the trance from Rama and Lakshuman and brought them to the temple. As directed by the goddess, they made an opening to one of the walls of the temple and pushed them in through it. Rama and Lakshuman were frightened at the sight of the goddess, who opened her mouth and said to them, "I shall now devour you, as I am very hungry; but before I do that, name the espouser of your cause." Whereupon the princes replied, "If Maruti were here, he would come to our rescue. We are now helpless, and throw ourselves on your mercy." Maruti was moved with pity at the princes, and immediately discovered himself to them. "I am now without weapons," said Rama, "and how can I kill the demons without them?" "You need not be afraid," continued Maruti, "I shall get your weapons here." So saying he brought the weapons and dhanushabans from Suvela. As princes were hungry, Maruti gave them to eat the butter and other things which he had preserved for them; and after they had appeased their hunger he sat in the place of the goddess, hiding them behind his back, and loudly exclaimed, "I am now ready to bless all my beloved demons one by one. Let Ahiravana come in first." Ahiravana was extremely glad, as the goddess wanted him first; and without loss of time he went in and stood before the deity, who trampled him under his foot and instantly killed him. As the demon did not come out for some time, the other demons outside the temple apprehended that there was some mischief in the temple, and began to make enquiries about him, when Maruti broke open the doors of the temple and killed a great number of the demons with his tail. Having been informed that his brother was killed by Maruti, Rama and Lakshuman, Mahiravana commenced to fight with them. He let off arrows after arrows at his enemies but they cut them off and let off an arrow and killed the demon with it; but, to their great surprise, they found that every drop of the blood of the demon produced one Mahiravana, and when Rama killed all the Mahiravanas produced by all the drops of the first Mahiravana the drops of so many Mahiravanas produced innumerable Mahiravanas and thus the more Rama killed the Mahiravanas, the more they were produced. At last Rama was confused, and did not know what to do. Maruti went and asked the Magari to acquaint him with the cause of the phenomenon. The Magari referred him to Chandraseni, wife of Ahiravana, and told him that she would tell him all about it. Whereupon Maruti called upon Chandraseni and implored her to tell him the cause of the phenomenon, when she said, " I shall be very glad to tell you the cause of the phenomenon, but unless Rama marries me, I shall not tell you the cause. I am charmed with the prince, and if you promise me that you will make him marry me, I shall tell you the cause." " Oh, yes. I can do it very easily," replied Maruti. " Then give me your promise," continued Chandraseni. Maruti gave his promise to her, when she said, " Ahiravana performed a severe penance on account of which the god, Siva, was pleased, and blessed him, saying that every drop of the nectar in the **kundas* in Patal, if mixed, with every drop of the blood of Mahiravana, it would produce one Mahiravana and that the drops of the blood of the Mahiravanas produced by such drops would multiply the Mahiravanas. So saying he presented the demon with a string of †*Bramahras* and told him that the Bramahras would supply his brother with the nectar at the time of a war. Now you see, these Bramahras, who are as big as mountains, go to Patal and sprinkle the nectar over the blood of the Mahiravanas and consequently there is no end to them. I, therefore, tell you to go to Patal and kill all the Bramahras, so that the nectar may not be sprinkled over the blood of the Mahiravanas killed by Rama." As soon as Maruti knew

* Holes in the ground. † Big black flies.

the secret, he immediately went to Patal and killed the Bramahras except their chief whose life was spared, because he promised the monkey that he would be useful to him on some occasion. Having killed the Bramahras, Maruti returned to Rama and told him to let off arrows at the Mahiravanas. The prince accordingly did it and killed all the Mahiravanas.

Immediately after this success Maruti remembered the promise given by him to Chandraseni and said to himself, "I do not know what I should do now. If I tell Rama to marry Chandraseni, he will never do so, because he has sworn that he will be faithful to his wife, Sita. If I fail to fulfil the promise given by me to her, she will curse me to death." Maruti however made bold and told Rama all about the promise given by him to Chandraseni. "I will not at all violate my oath." replied Rama, "If you like, I can come to the place of Chandraseni and bless her." "Yes," continued Maruti, "you can do so." Thence Maruti first came alone to Chandraseni and said to her, "Rama will come to-night. Keep your **manchaka* ready for him, but I tell you one thing that if the manchaka is broken by the weight of Rama, he will never marry you and will go directly home. I therefore, tell you to order a strong manchaka to be made." Chandraseni got a strong and beautiful manchaka ready for Rama and sat there expecting the prince. Maruti sent the chief of the Bramahra without her knowledge to hollow the bed-stead in such a manner that as soon as Rama sat on it, it would be broken to pieces. The Bramahra skilfully hollowed the whole of the manchaka with his sting and went away. In the evening Maruti, accompanied by Rama, came to Chandraseni, who received him and made him sit on the manchaka; but no sooner did Rama sit on it than it was broken to pieces. Whereupon Rama

* A bed-stead.

immediately got up and began to walk towards his place, accompanied by Maruti, when Chandraseni indignantly exclaimed, "Ah, monkey! Thou art a great scoundrel. This is thy dodge. I will now curse thee to death." Maruti was alarmed, when Rama went and pacified her, saying that he would marry her during his another incarnation and that she would be called Satyabhama. After all the demons were killed, Rama gave Mahikavati to Makardwaja and returned to Suvela with Maruti and the other monkeys.

On the return of Rama to Suvela Ravan said to his courtiers, "There is no use of my living in this world without my beloved son, Indrajit. I must now either kill Rama or kill myself." So saying he commenced to let off arrows at Rama which the latter cut off. But the prince was struck with one arrow, when Vibhishan let off arrows at the demon-king, who boiled with rage, discharged at his brother a weapon called Bramahshakti. Lakshuman immediately cut it off, when Ravana discharged another powerful weapon at the prince but Maruti caught hold of it before it struck him. To the great surprise of all, the weapon became a female in the hands of Maruti and said to him, "Well, Maruti, you say that you are a Brahmachari and how do you touch a female? You will be sinful, if you do not let me go." Maruti was greatly astonished at the female in his hands; and as soon as she uttered the word, 'sin,' he placed her on the ground, when she immediately became a weapon and, rushing upon Lakshuman, struck his head and chest; and consequently he fell down lifeless. Rama and all the monkeys were alarmed, and much lamented for him. Ravana, elate with the success, returned to Lanka with exultation. Rama and the monkeys were in confusion, and did not know what to do. All were discouraged, and thought of leaving Suvela. Shortly after, Ravana again came to fight, when Rama, boiled with rage, let off arrows at him and the other demons and killed many of them. The demon-king, being unable to overcome him, trembled from head to foot. He became mad and the picture of Rama presented itself before him wherever he went. Having been frightened, he immediately returned to Lanka and told his wife, Mandodari, about it, when she said, "My love, my dearest, even now restore Sita to Rama and be his friend." "No, no," Ravana indignantly replied, "that can never be done. I will either kill myself or kill Rama." Immediately after Mandodari had returned to her palace, he ordered the demons to dig an excavation in the ground. The excavation was accordingly dug; and in that excavation he performed a penance to get a divya ratha from the god of fire and sat there in deep meditation.

Rama grieved for his brother, and all the monkeys were alarmed. In the meantime, their physician, Susena, felt the pulse of Lakshuman and said, "Lakshuman has still life in him and he will be no more, as soon as the sun rises in the morning. If the plant of nectar is brought here from Dronagiri in the course of the night, Lakshuman can be restored to life. Is there any warrior who can go forty millions of yojans from this place and get the plant here in the course of the night?" As soon as the physician put the question, Maruti said, "I will just go and bring Dronagiri here in three hours." So saying he took his leave of Rama and jumped from Suvela. He came to a hill called Madaranchela which was close to Dronagiri. Maruti was very thirsty; and to refresh himself he went to the abode of an old Brahman and requested him for a cup of water. This Brahman, who had a number of disciples with him, blessed Maruti and said, "I am very glad to see you here. Kindly spend this night with us here and go in the morning." "I can not wait here for a minute," replied Maruti. "I must do my business as soon as possible." When the Brahman found that Maruti did not comply with his wishes, he showed him a river. Maruti went there and stooped to take water, when a *vivasi** as big as a mountain came out to devour the monkey, who at once seized her by her legs and instantly killed her. When she was killed, a beautiful *devangana*† came out of her belly and threw herself at the feet of Maruti. She said, " I was very beautiful; and, being proud of my beauty, I laughed at a sage, who got indignant and cursed me, saying that I would be a vivasi. I implored him to look upon me with mercy and make the curse a little milder, when he said that I would be released from the curse by your hands. I also inform you that the Brahman, who lives in that abode, is a demon called Kalnemi. He has been here for many days with his companions, who are also demons. Ravana has sent this demon to detain you here, and when you refused to comply with his wishes, he told you to go to that river in order that I might devour you." No sooner did the devangana inform Maruti of this than he came back to the abode of the Brahman, when the latter said to the monkey, " You ought to give me some presents, as I have pointed out the river to you." " I shall be very glad to give you presents," replied Maruti. The demon stared at the monkey, when the latter gave him blows as precious presents from him. The demon immediately assumed his original form which was five yojans in length and breadth, and combated with Maruti but the latter instantly killed him; and his companions fled to Lanka to inform Ravana of it. Maruti then went to Dronagiri and implored him to accompany him to Suvela, when the mountain said, " Thou art a troublesome creature. Go away. Thou, fool. I will never come with thee." Maruti got enraged and, having lifted up the mountain with his tail, set out for Suvela. But on the road Bharat, the

* A goddess. † A courtesan of heaven.

third brother of Rama, who was living at Nandigram with the Rishi, Vashista, having looked at the bright and glittering mountain and, having thought that it was some thing to entrap Rama and Lakshuman, let off an arrow at it, which passed through the mountain and pierced an arm of Maruti. The monkey, having been wounded, immediately came down with the mountain, repeating, all the time, the name of Rama. Bharat heard the repetition of the name of Rama and asked him who he was, when the monkey informed him of what had happened to Lakshuman and said, " What should I do now? How can I go to Suvela before the sunrise. If I do not reach Suvela with this mountain in the course of the night, Lakshuman will be no more." " You need not be afraid," replied Bharat. " I shall send you and the mountain to Suvela, in a minute, though it is at a distance of thousands of yojans from this place. Just sit on the top of my arrow, which will carry you and the mountain there in a minute" Maruti was surprised at the valour and power of Bharat, and continued, " You need not take so much trouble. I can do it myself." So saying he took his leave of the prince and jumped from Nandigram with the mountain and came to Suvela. The physician immediately came and, taking out the juice of the plant of nectar, applied it to Lakshuman and brought him to life. In like manner he applied the juice to all the monkeys killed by Ravana and restored them to life. This having been done, Maruti took the mountain and placed it where it formerly stood. Ravana however despatched one hundred demons to snatch Dronagiri from the hands of Maruti but the latter, holding the mountain in his one hand, killed them all with his other hand.

Rama, Lakshuman, and the monkeys again prepared themselves to fight with Ravana but the demon-king did not come out of Lanka for some time. In the meantime

Vibhishan came and said to Rama, " Ravana is performing a penance like that which was done by Indrajit and half of the divyaratha has come out of fire. Unless you send some monkey-warriors there and destroy the havan made by him, you will not be able to overcome him." No sooner did Vibhishan inform Rama of this than the latter despatched Maruti, Nala, Nila, Sugriva, and other monkeys to Lanka. They all went and searched the place where the demon-king was performing the penance; but they could not find out the place. But, in the mean-time, Sharma, wife of Vibhishan, showed the place to them. Whereupon they went to the mouth of the excavation and, having removed the stone which was placed upon it, rushed into it, when Ravana was in deep meditation. The monkeys, having destroyed the havan and the ratha, tried their utmost to arouse him from his meditation but they failed to do so. They struck him with their weapons, they threw rock and trees upon him, they gave blows to him but all was in vain. At last Sugriva caught hold of Mandodari and brought her in the excavation. She was frightened, and violently cried. Her yell aroused the demon-king from meditation; and as soon as he saw his wife there, and having found that the havan was destroyed by the monkeys, he was greatly enraged and beat them all down. The monkeys immediately returned to Suvela leaving Ravana and his wife in the excavation. The demon-king said to Mandodari " My dearest, do not grieve for what has happened to you. Pain and pleasure are made for us mortal beings and we must experience them according to their turns. Now I am going to fight with Rama. I will either kill myself or kill Rama. If I return to you, it is all right; and if I be killed, these are the last words I address to you." So saying the demon-king took the remaining demons with him and commenced operations, when all the monkeys threw at him innumerable mountains, rocks, and trees but Ravana cut them off in no time and beat them all down. Finding that Ravana could not be overcome by the monkeys, Rama immediately attacked him, when the demon-king let off a serpent-weapon, which produced innumerable serpents and stung the monkeys. Rama let off a Garuda-weapon, which produced garudas and killed all the serpents. Rama let off a rain-weapon, which produced the rain and flowed the demons, when Ravana let off a wind-weapon, which produced the wind and dispersed the rain. Rama let off a mountain-weapon, which produced mountains and stopped the wind. Ravana let off a diamond-weapon, which produced diamonds and broke all the mountains. Ravana let off innumerable arrows at Rama at one and the same time but the latter cut them off with one arrow. Ravana then let off a very powerful arrow, which struck Rama and passed through his left foot, when all the monkeys got enraged and began to throw arrows, rocks, and trees at Ravana but the latter bravely broke them with his weapons. Ravana fought from his chariot and Rama from the ground. Finding that the prince was in a bad position, Indra, the chief of the gods in heaven, sent his chariot for him, which he mounted and began to fight with his enemy. They both were very powerful and fought with each other for seven days and seven nights without cessation. Rama then let off four arrows and killed the horses of Ravana. The demon-king then immediately put other horses to his chariot, when Rama let off an arrow of the size of the half moon, which Ravana cut off with the like arrow. Whereupon Rama let off a sharp weapon, which struck the chest of the demon-king and cut off his ten heads but, to the surprise of all, the heads again fixed themselves to him. Rama again cut them off but they again fixed themselves to Ravana. Rama having failed to separate the heads from

Ravana, all the monkeys were alarmed, when the charioteer, Matuli, said to Rama, " Ravana has got a phial full of nectar in his breast. Just let off an arrow at his breast and break the phial, so that the heads will not fix themselves to the demon-king over and over again." Hearing this from Matuli Rama discharged a powerful weapon called Agasti Data and broke the phial in his breast; and immediately after, he cut off his ten heads and killed him on the spot. Vibhishan lamented for his brother the demon-king, when Rama consoled and pacified him. Mandodari and his other wives came and violently cried for their husband. Vibhishan consoled them and sent them to their palaces. The funeral ceremony of Ravana was then performed by his brother; and soon after, Rama installed him in the throne of Lanka. All the demons acknowledged him as their king and paid homage to him. All the gods and kings imprisoned by Ravana, were released from the prison there. Rama visited them all and heartily embraced them. Rama then asked Maruti and Vibhishan to bring Sita from the Asoka forest. Whereupon they immediately went to the forest and informed her of what had happened to Ravana and said to her, " We are desired by Rama to bring you to Suvela. Please, therefore, prepare yourself to accompany us." Sita having prepared herself to accompany them, Vibhishan seated her in a **sibika* and brought her to Suvela. She went to embrace Rama affectionately, when the latter said to her, " Do not come near me. I have set you at liberty in order that the people may not call me cruel. You have been for so many years in Lanka, and I do not know what you hava done during that time. I can not now admit you into my house; you can go wherever you like. I have no objection to it whatsoever." Hearing these words from Rama Sita was over-whelmed

* A planquin.

with grief, and replied, "I am unfortunate. For nothing you have taken trouble for me. For nothing you have given trouble to all the monkeys. If you do not like to admit me into your house, take your sword and cut off my head. I have led a pious and moral life, and I shall presently satisfy you about it." Having addressed these words to Rama, she requested all the monkeys to arrange a pile of wood and set fire to it. All the monkeys accordingly arranged a pile and set fire to it. Sita went near it and loudly exclaimed in the presence of all the monkeys and demons, "All know that I was carried off and detained by Ravana. I say that I led a pious and moral life during the time I was in the kingdom of the demon. There is the fire ready to receive me. I shall now throw myself into it; and if what I say is false, I shall be burnt in it. And if what I say is true, I shall come out of the fire unhurt." So saying Sita threw herself into the fire and disappeared for about three hours. Rama, Lakshuman, and all the monkeys grieved for her and stood near the pile bewildered. But, in the meantime, the god of fire brought her out of it, well decorated with ornaments, and gave her in charge of Rama, who heartily embraced her.

Shortly after, Rama set out for Ayodya in a beautiful *viman.** Sugriva, Vibhishan, all the monkeys, and demons were seated in it. On the road Rama visited the Rishis and his other friends, who had supported him in the forest, and directly came to Nandigram, where he alighted from the viman and saw his brother, Bharat, who heartily embraced him with tears of joy. Rama then sent the viman back and stayed in the forest of Nandigram, with Sugriva, Vibhishan, all the monkeys and demons. In the meantime, Shatrughna and Sumant came to the

* A chariot of the gods serving as a throne or as a conveyance through the skies, self-directed and self-moving.

forest with all their army and saw Rama, Lakshuman, and Sita. Kausalya, Sumitra, and Kayakayi also came there and affectionately embraced their sons. Kayakayi remembered her past conduct towards Rama and repented of what she had done to ruin him. They all then seated themselves in chariots and came to Ayodya with the acclamation of joy.

On the return of Rama from Suvela all the kings on earth including his father-in-law, Janaka, saw him. All the people of Ayodya were exceedingly glad to see Rama, Lakshuman, and Sita. Rama entertained all the kings, Rishis, demons, and monkeys for some days. Sita affectionately embraced her sister and her all relations. Soon after, Rama was installed by the Rishi, Vashista, in the throne of Ayodya, when all the kings paid tribute to him. Immediately after the ceremony of installation was over, Rama gave presents to Sugriva, Vibhishan and all other kings. But Maruti did not accept any of the presents, as the other monkeys did. The monkeys asked Maruti why he refused the presents from Rama. "Why do I want the presents from Rama?" replied Maruti. "Rama is always in my heart." Whereupon the monkeys continued, "If what you say is true, show us Rama in your heart." As soon as the monkeys uttered these words, Maruti ripped his heart and showed Rama to them from within. The monkeys were greatly surprised, and threw themselves at the feet of Maruti. When Rama was on the throne, Kayakayi peeped at him through a window and said, "My son is unfortunate. Look at Rama, how he is happy. I tried my utmost to get the throne for him but he did not listen to me. And at last he has become a slave of his brother, Rama." Vashista overheard what she had said and replied, "I told you many things but you would never mind me. It was owing to your own folly and jealousy that Rama was sent to the forest, and it was you who killed your husband, Dasharatha. I now still advise you to be a good woman and trust, you will love Rama and Lakshuman as your sons, Bharat and Shatrughna." Soon after, Rama, Sugriva, Vibhishan, and all other kings returned to their respective armies. Only Maruti always remained with Rama. Rama reigned in Ayodya for eleven thousand years and all his subjects were happy under his reign and led a very pious life.

Sita was in the farmily way for the first time, and when she passed six months, Rama took her to his pleasant garden, where they spent some time in pleasure. While they were there, Rama said to Sita, "My sweet heart, you have now passed six months of your pregnancy. Just let me know what you like to enjoy. I am ready to gratify any of your desires." "My love, what I want to enjoy is this," replied Sita, "that you and I should go to a forest where Rishis live, and eat *kandamuls*† there, and sleep on the bed of *Trana*‡ on the ground." When Sita expressed her desire, he said to himself, "Lo, she suffered so much in the forest and yet she likes to go to a forest." So saying to himself he returned home with her. A few days before Rama went to the garden he had ordered his officers to go round the city at night and hear whether his subjects spoke ill of him. The officers, who had gone round the city, came to Rama and said to him, "We went to every door successively for some days and found that all your subjects spoke well of you except one washerman called, Rajaka, who scandalized you. One day this Rajaka beat his wife, and consequently she ran to her parents' house without his knowledge. Her father intervened and came to the house of his son-in-law with his daughter and requested him to admit her into his house, when Rajaka said, 'I will never admit her into my house. I am not that Rama,

† Esculent roots. ‡ Grass.

who shamelessly admitted Sita into his house, though she lived under the roof of Ravana for many years. I am a pure washerman. I am the man who clean and remove the dirt and spots on the dresses and clothes of the people, and do you mean to say that I will admit your unclean daughter again into my house? You can take her back. I do not wish to see her face.' This is the only man who has scandalized you." As soon as Rama heard these words from the officers, he became exceedingly sorry and, having called Lakshuman, said to him, "You see, my brother, that Rajaka has scandalized me, though Sita is faithful and as pious as any thing. That wicked washerman has scandalized me, because I have admitted her into my house. I cannot bear this at all. I, therefore, bade you take Sita to the yonder forest and, leaving her there alone, return to me as soon as possible." "You need not take to your heart what Rajaka has said about you," replied Lakshuman. "There are many wicked persons who are in the habit of scandalizing others. As a wise and prudent man you should not mind it. Let the people say whatever they like. Why do you mind that stupid man? I shall cut off his tongue." "What you say is right," continued Rama, "but if you cut off the tongue of that man, the people will say that we are guilty. It is, therefore, far better, if we get rid of Sita, so that nobody may speak ill of us." Lakshuman hesitated to comply with his wishes, when Rama exclaimed, "If you do not obey me, I shall kill myself on this spot." Finding that Rama was serious, Lakshuman immediately got up and entered the room of Sita, who kindly received him and made him sit with her. Lakshuman said to her, "Rama has told me to take you to the yonder forest as soon as possible. So, kindly prepare yourself and accompany me there." "Has Rama told you to take me to the forest?" replied she. "Ah! I am very fortunate. Some days ago he asked me what I wanted to enjoy, and I told him that I liked to pass four or five days in a forest, eat kandamuls there and sleep on the bed of trana. I think, for the same purpose he is going to send me with you. Let us start. I am quite ready." Listening to what Sita had said Lakshuman felt much and shed tears for her. Soon after, Lakshuman seated her in a chariot near the river, Janavi, and began to drive it, when she observed bad omens and asked him what those omens indicated. Lakshuman, overwhelmed with grief, could not utter a syllable and quietly drove the chariot. When she found him quiet and in grief, she said to him, "Why are you so sorry? Why don't you speak with me?" Lakshuman still kept quiet and, crossing the river in a boat, landed her in the forest, where there was no human being and it was inhabited by lions, serpents, tigers, and other animals. She asked Lakshuman, "Where are the abodes of Rishis?" Lakshuman did not reply; but, making a bed of grass, he seated her on it. He then fell at her feet and said with tears in his eyes, "Mother, Rama has left you alone in this forest. I have brought you here, as I could not disobey him." No sooner did Lakshuman speak these words than she fainted. While she was insensible, Lakshuman prayed to the goddess of the forest and every creature in it to protect her and started for Ayodya. When he went some paces off, Sita came to herself and, standing on her legs, loudly exclaimed, "O! Lakshuman, kindly return and take me back. Why do you leave me here without any faults on my part? Kill me and tell Rama of it. Where shall I go in this dreary forest." So saying she violently cried so much so that even trees and stones shed tears for her. Lakshuman returned to Ayodya and told Rama all about Sita. Sita wandered in the forest barefooted. She had no shelter there. She often fainted. She said to herself, "It is now useless to live in this world. I should have killed myself but I can not do so. If I kill myself, I shall be guilty of suicide and murder, because the infant child in my womb will also be killed with me." So saying to herself she abandoned the idea of killing herself. In the meantime, the Rishi, Valmika, having heard the yells of Sita, came up to her and said, "Who are you? What has brought you here?" "I am a daughter of Janak and wife of Rama," replied Sita. Lakshuman left me alone in this dreary forest without any faults on my part. I am quite a stranger here. So I implore you to be my father." "My name is Valmika," replied Valmika." Rama knows me well. Your father, Janak, is my friend; and therefore, I look upon you as my daughter. Two sons will be born to you. They will be more powerful than their father, and will revenge themselves upon those who have left you alone in this forest without any faults on your part." Valmika then led Sita to his abode, when all the Rishis gathered around him and asked him, "Who is this woman?" "This is Sita," replied Valmika. "Why have you brought her here? Surely you will get into difficulties on account of her," continued the Rishis. One of the Rishis said, "If she is Sita, tell her to bring that river here." Sita prayed to the river, and it flowed where she was standing. The Rishis were alarmed, and prayed to her for protection. She again prayed to the river and sent her back. Valmika brought Sita to his abode and took every care of her. After the expiration of nine months, she was delivered of twin sons at midday as bright as the sun, when the wives of the Rishis came and helped her in her confinement. The first born son was the younger and the second born was the eldest. The disciples of Valmika went and informed the Rishi of the birth of the two sons. Whereupon Valmika immediately came to his abcde and performed the necessary ceremony. He sprinkled water over the younger son with a *kusha** and named him Kusha after it. The eldest son having been placed on *lavas*,† the Rishi, in like manner, sprinkled the water over him and called him Lahu. When the two sons became eight years old, the Rishi performed their *Vrataband*‡ and entertained the Rishis for four days. A kamdhenu or a cow supplied them with whatever they wanted. The Rishi taught them the Vedas, mantras, Ramayan, the Purans and *dhanurvidya.*§ They thoroughly mastered all sciences and arts and always played with the sons of the Rishis. When they became ten years old, they went on hunting excursions and brought home the animals killed by them. One day Kusha killed a sage on the top of a mountain, who was a brother of Valmika. He was meditating there in the form of a deer. They dragged the corpse of the sage towards the abode of Valmika, when the latter asked them on the road what they were doing. "We have brought a deer for you" replied they, "and shall make a seat of its skins for you." Valamika, having looked at the corpse, found that it was his brother and said to himself "Now both the boys have become very brave. They have even killed a Brahman." So saying to himself Valmika performed the funeral ceremony of his brother and informed Sita of the valour of her sons, when she said, "What do I know? It is you who have taught them dhanurvidya, mantras, arts, and all sciences. I implore you, Papa, to free them from the sin." "Unless they bring one thousand *Brahma Kamals*,"¶ replied Valmika, "and worship the god, Siva, with all their heart and soul, they will not be freed from the sin." "Papa, will you kindly tell us where those kamals can be had?" enquired the boys. "We will

---

* Grass. † A rush-like grass. ‡ The ceremony of invesiting a boy with a thread § The art of using a bow and an arrow ¶ Lotuses.

immediately bring them here." "There is a lake called Brahmasarovar near Ayodya," continued Valmika, "but a number of warriors are posted by Rama to watch it. Those kamals are used by Rama for the worship of Siva." "Pooh!" said the boys, "We shall immediately bring those kamals. Let there be hundreds of brave warriors to watch the lake, we shall punish them and even capture Rama." So saying they hastened to the lake. Kusha went and plucked all the kamals, when the warriors came upon him; but Lahu killed many of them. Those who had escaped, went and informed Rama of what the boys had done. Rama was greatly surprised, and praised the valour of the boys. Lahu and Kusha brought the kamals and worshipped Siva as directed by Valmika, and thus they were freed from the sin they had committed in killing the Brahman. One day, while both the boys were shampooing the feet of their mother, Kusha asked her, "In what country we were born? What is the name of the country and what is our race and who is our father?" "Rama, Lakshuman, Bharat and Shatrughna" replied Sita, "are sons of Dasharatha, who was the king of Ayodya and belonged to the solar race. Rama, the eldest son of the king, is your father. I am left in this forest alone, because a washerman scandalized your father on my account." So saying she shed tears, when both the boys got much enraged at Rama and consoled their mother. Owing to the injustice done by Rama to Sita there was a terrible famine in Ayodya for twelve years. The people and animals suffered much. The rain fell in torrents. Rama was alarmed and asked the Rishi, Vashista, what the cause of the famine was, when the latter replied, "You have unjustly left Sita in the forest, although she is a paragon of virtue; and this is the cause of the famine. In order to put it down you must celebrate an *Ashwamedha* *." Whereupon Rama

* With a view to be an emperor or to free himself from sin

erected a *mandap* * on the bank of the river, Sharayu, one yojan in length, and invited all kings to that ceremony including Vibhishan, Sugriva, Nala, Nila, Maruti, Sharab, Govaksha, and all other monkeys. Rama, having performed the necessary ceremony, brought the best horse called *shamakarna* † from his stable and made it stand in the mandap. Vashista tied up to its forehead a golden *Patrika* ‡ and wrote on it the following words:—" Rama, the king of Ayodya, son of Dasharatha, has let the shamakarna loose. It is guarded by six billions of warriors under the command of Shatrughna, and any king, who is powerful and mighty, is required to capture the horse and fight with its owner, but if he is unable to do so, he must submit to Rama and pay tribute to him." Rama worshipped the shamakarna and appointed Shatrughna as commander-in-chief of the six billions of the warriors who followed the horse. Rama performed the necessary *yadnya* § for many days in the mandap strongly guarded by Sugriva, Vibhishan, and Maruti. Lakshuman, Bharat, and Sumant supplied him with all the necessary things for the purpose.

Shatrughna conquered fifty six kings of very large countries, who submitted to him and, having paid tribute to Rama, followed the prince. The shamakarna of Rama began to gallop on the road on which the abode of Valmika

---

a monarch would let a horse loose with a patrika or letter on its fore-head stating that any monarch whose dominion the animal entered, should either catch it and fight with its master or submit to him and give him tribute. Wherever this animal entered, it was accompanied by the monarch with large armies. Monarchs read the patrika and fought with the invading monarch, if they were powerful to do so ; and if not, they gave him tribute. After all the monarchs were subdued, the horse was either killed or let go alive, and hence it is called ashwamedha or horse-sacrifice

* A horse. † An open shade or hall. ‡ A letter. § A sacrifice.

stood. The Rishi, Valmika, had gone to Patal to be present at the yadnya performed by Varun. Before he left for Patal, he had told the boys to watch his abode in his absence. Both the small boys were playing together with other playmates near the abode at the time the shamakarna galloped, when Lahu showed the animal to his playmates and, having pulled off the patrika from the head of the horse, read the contents of it. He laughed at what he had read, and said, "Is Rama only a mighty king on earth? Pooh! I shall capture this horse, and let me see who will fight with me and recover the horse." So saying he tied up the animal to a plantain-tree. All the children of the Rishis were alarmed and said, "No doubt this horse belongs to a king. How dare you capture the animal? If the king come here and ask us who has detained the horse, we will surely give your name." In the meantime, some of the warriors came there and, looking at the children of the Rishis, said, "Who are you? Who has tied up the horse to the plantain-tree?" "We do not know anything about it," replied the children. "There stands the boy who has tied up the horse to the tree and he will tell you why he has done so." In the meantime, Shatrughna and all other warriors reached there. Looking at the tenderness of Lahu they coaxed him and went to untie the horse, when the former loudly exclaimed, "I did capture the horse. I stand here to fight with you. Who is your Rama? Go and tell him that I am ready to fight with him. You say that I am a child but I will kill you all and put down your pride." The warriors said to themselves, "It is unbecoming on our part to fight with these tender boys. All the kings will laugh at us, if we fight with them. It is far better to untie the horse and walk quietly." So saying all the warriors went to untie the animal, when Lahu let off arrows and cut off the hands of those who went to untie the horse. All the six billions of warriors at once rushed upon the boy, who let off arrows and defeated them with heavy loss, when Shatrughna drove his chariot but there was no room to move it, as there were heaps of the corpses of the warriors killed by Lahu. He however pushed aside the corpses and went where the boy was standing. Finding him just like Rama, he asked him, "Whose child you are? You have killed all my warriors. I shall now severely punish you." "Very well, I shall see how you will save your life now," replied Lahu. Shatrughna got enraged and let off an arrow at the boy, who cut it off in no time. He then let off many arrows which Lahu cut off and struck the former with his arrows. At last he threw at Lahu the deadly arrow given by Rama to him for use in difficulty, when Lahu said, "I do not know how to cut off this arrow. Kusha has a knowledge of it. If he had not gone to the forest for kandamuls, he would have cut it off." Lahu however let off a fiery arrow and cut off a part of the deadly arrow but the remaining half of it struck the boy; and consequently he fell insensible on the ground. Shatrughna was moved, and having gone near the boy, looked at him attentively. He resembled Rama. Shatrughna applied water to his eyes and brought to his senses; and in order to show him to Rama he put him into his chariot and proceeded further with the shamakarna. The children ran and informed Sita of the fate of her son, Lahu, when she fainted and, coming to herself, violently cried. She exclaimed with grief, "I am helpless and very unfortunate. Which heartless man has seized my child? O! my son, thou art tender. Thou must have been wounded. Thy eyes must have been broken by the arrows of the enemy. My children are too young. They live upon kandamuls and how will they be strong enough to fight with warriors? Those who raise a weapon against a child, are not Kshatriyas. How is it that nobody felt pity at the child? Who has carried off the little wealth I had? Who has carried off the stick of a blind and lame woman? If my father, Valmika, were here, he would go to his rescue, but unfortunately he has gone to patal. Kusha has also gone to the forest, what shall I do now? Who will get my son back." In the meantime, Kusha returned from the forest and asked his mother where his brother was, when she, with tears in her eyes, informed him of what had happened to Lahu. As soon as he was informed of the fate of his brother, he took up his bow and arrow and ran after Shatrughna and the other warriors. Kusha called out and said, "Who are you, thieves. Where are you going to take the stolen thing?" So saying he let off arrows at the army of Shatrughna, when the latter turned round and loudly said, "Child, I shall immediately seize and carry you off with us." So saying Shatrughna let off ten arrows at Kusha, which the latter cut off and broke the chariot and killed the four horses of the former with nine arrows; and with three arrows his helmet and *chap* * were broken. Shatrughna fell on the ground and combated with Kusha, when the latter let off two arrows and cut off his two hands; and at the same time his head was cut off with another arrow. On the fall of Shatrughna his brother, Nagendranath, let off twenty arrows at the boy but the latter broke off the arrows with one arrow and cut off the head of Nagendranath with an arrow of the size of the half moon. Having done this, he continued the letting off arrows at the warriors, who could not overcome Kusha. The boy killed many billions of warriors and all the kings who had submitted to Rama. Kusha then went and searched his brother, whom he found in the chariot of Shatrughna. He was insensible. Kusha brought him to senses and embraced him affectionately. Lahu said, "Let us now go home with the shamakarna."

* Bow.

"I am sure, many other warriors will come here to fight with us," replied Kusha. "It is not safe to return home. Let us kill all who will come here to take the horse, and then return home." A few wounded warriors went and informed Rama that Shatrughna and six billions of the warriors were killed by two small boys of a Rishi. Rama was alarmed at the news and immediately despatched Lakshuman with a large army to the seat of the war. He, looking at the beautiful boys of the age of twelve years, was greatly surprised at their bravery. The warriors said, "Capture, capture the boys. Where will they go now?" The boys prayed to the sun, who was pleased with them and presented them with a successful weapon, which Lahu took up and attacked the warriors of Lakshuman and killed a large number of them, when Lakshuman said to Kalajit, "As long as the two boys stand together, nobody can overcome them. Let us, therefore, separate them both and seize them." So saying Lakshuman separated the boys with the assistance of all his warriors but Lahu let off one arrow, which produced kotis of arrows and killed the warriors. Finding Lakshuman in a bad position a demon called Rudhi, a great friend of Rama, jumping into the air, came down where Lahu was standing, and snatched the weapon from his hands and flew like a bird, when Lahu also flew with him and, seizing the demon by his hair and turning him like a wheel, flung him down and instantly killed him. Lakshuman got enraged and let off at the two boys five arrows as powerful as lightning, which Lahu cut off in a minute. Lahu said to Lakshuman, "You formerly killed Indrajit. Let me see your valour now. You fasted for fourteen years. No doubt you must have now rest and I shall just give it to you." "What is the name of your father?" asked Lakshuman. "Why do you want to know it?" replied Lahu. "Come on, let us now fight." So saying he let off one arrow and threw Lakshuman with his chariot into the sky, which turned in the air and came down on the ground. Lakshuman mounted another chariot and continued letting off arrows at Lahu, which the latter cut off one after another in the twinkle of an eye. Lakshuman then let off an arrow, which produced kotis of * *gadas*, when Lahu made use of the mantra given by Valmika, which produced koits of † *chakras* and cut off the gadas. Lakshuman then let off a mountain-weapon, which produced mountains but Lahu broke them with the diamonds produced by a diamond-weapon. Thus Lakshuman tried his utmost to kill Lahu with his arrows but he could not overcome the boy, when the latter said to him, " Why have you stopped now ? If your arrows are finished, go back and call your Rama." Lakshuman did not reply to what Lahu had said, and indignantly let off arrows at Lahu, when the latter let off a melody-weapon, which produced melodious sounds and charmed Lakshuman, who was an incarnation of the serpent, Shesha. Lakshuman, having been charmed with the melodious sounds, ceased to fight and began to nod his head with mirth.

Kalajit surrounded Kusha with his troops but the latter killed them all and joined his brother. Rama was about to send Bharat with more troops to re-enforce the army of Lakshuman with instructions to Lakshuman that they should put upon the boys a fascination-weapon and, seizing the two boys, bring them to him alive, so that their mother might not cry for them. But in the meantime, a few wounded warriors went and informed Rama that Lakshuman had fallen in the field of war with Kalajit and all the warriors commanded by him. Rama, hearing this, grieved much for Lakshuman and immediately despatched Maruti and Bharat with more warriors. When Bharat saw the boys just like Rama, he said to Maruti, " There is no doubt that the boys are sons of Rama." " I should think so," replied Maruti. Lahu and Kusha saw them whisper to each other and said, "No doubt they will engage us in conversation and take the shamakarna from us." Kusha told Lahu to watch the horse and he himself came up to Bharat and asked him, "You are, I suppose, elder than Lakshuman. Are you not? You seem to be a brave soldier." "Just tell me what is your name, who your parents are, and tell me with whom you fought before?" "My name is Kusha," replied the child. "Depart from this place," continued Bharat, "and tell your mother that I have spared your life." "I think, Rama has sent you here to capture us," said Kusha. "I now tell you, either fight with me or depart from this place as soon as you can. I do not pursue you. Just go and get your Rama here." Bharat got enraged and let off various arrows and weapons at Kusha, which the latter cut off very easily. At last he let off a diamond-weapon at Maruti, and made him insensible. This news having been communicated to Rama, the latter mounted his chariot and personally came to the field of the war with the army of the monkeys. The monkeys threw at the boys mountains, rocks and trees which they broke with their weapons and killed many monkey-warriors, and some monkeys fled for fear of life. At this time Maruti jumped into the air to lift up the boys with his tail but Kusha, perceiving his intention, let off a powerful arrow at him, which struck the monkey and brought him down. Kusha loudly said "Oh! ugly monkey. You destroyed the Asoka forest but here you cannot do any thing. The throwing of stones and mountains at demons was not a war. There is no Dronagiri here. You jumped over the sea and burnt Lanka. There is nothing like that here." In the meantime, Sugriva threw trees at the boys but Lahu cut them off, and made Sugriva, Nila, Jambuvant, Angad and Maruti and other monkeys insensible. Looking at this defeat Rama let off arrows at

See Page 75.
MARUTI
NALA
RAVANA
MANDODARI
SUGRIVA
See Page 93
ARMY
LAHU
KUSHA
See Page 94
SITA
LAHU
KUSHA
VALMIKA
MAR.
RAMA

the two boys which the latter cut off and let off innumerable arrows, which scattered throughout the sky without hurting Rama. Looking at the bravery of the boys Rama asked, "Children of the Rishis, listen to me, I shall give you what you want. I shall give you a cow, which will give you milk. I am pleased with you and will give you whatever you want." "We want nothing from you," replied the boys, "but on the contrary we will give you whatever you want. You can enjoy your own wealth. We have heard enough of you. You are such a heartless and cruel man that no one like you can be found on this earth. Sita, an innocent woman of virtue, you left alone in the forest. This is most wicked on your part" Listening to what they had said, Rama was moved with affection for them and thought of stroking their heads with tenderness. But the boys told him to continue fighting with them. "Just tell me," said Rama, "Who you are, who your parents are, which guru gave you education, who taught you dhanurvidya, science, arts and mantras?" The boys heartily laughed and said, "This man does not feel for his brothers. He wants us to tell him stories. Sir, first fight with us and then ask us stories. You have killed Ravana and done many brave acts. Now let us see a little of it. We shall never allow you to depart from this place without fighting with us. If you cannot fight with us, return home quietly or be a * *sanyasi*, because you have neither wife, nor children." Rama asked, "Tell me who you are, and then I shall fight with you." In the meantime, a voice in the sky said, "Rama, do not fight. The boys are your sons." As soon as Rama heard what the voice had said, he fell down insensible. Kusha came up to him and, taking off his mugut, put it on his own head. Lahu stripped Lakshuman of his ornaments and wore them himself. Having done this, they mounted the chariot of Rama and

* An ascetic.

tying up Maruti, Sugriva, Angad, Jambuvant and other monkeys to the chariot for the amusement of their mother, drove to their abode. They told Sita that they had made Rama and his brothers insensible in the field of war and killed all their warriors. "Here are the monkeys," said they, "we have brought for your amusement." Sita knew them and did not come out, because they might feel ashamed of their state. She said to her sons, "Let the monkeys go away. We shall never keep them here." The boys then went and untied them. The monkeys came and informed Rama of what they had seen. In the meantime, Valmika returned from Patal; and, having been informed of what had happened, he went and brought all the warriors to life by sprinkling water over them from his * *Kamandalu*. The Rishi then gave the two boys and Sita in charge of Rama, who heartily embraced them. Shortly after, Rama took leave of Valmika and returned to Ayodya with his sons and completed the ashwamedha.

* The water pot used by an ascetic and religious student.

THE END.